Praise God I'm Saved, "Now What?"

By

Dr. Todd Zike

ISBN 978-1-940609-15-7 Softcover

Teachers Book

This book was printed in the United States of America.
To order additional copies of this book, contact:

Eagles Nest Ministry
Dr. Todd Zike
P.O. Box 19
Blanchester, OH 45107
513-785-9945

Published by FWB Publications

FWB

The Bible Believers'
Basic
Bible Study

"But grow in the grace, and in the knowledge of our Lord and Saviour Jesus Christ, to Him be glory both now and forever. Amen." (II Peter 3:18)

Dr. Todd Br. Zike

Preface

This book of basic Bible teaching is a must for every Christian student, and family to get a deeper knowledge of the things of God in this present generation. The Word of God is the only hope for the world. This book will help you to grasp the truth in depth of these Bible doctrines in a simple, quick, yet an in-depth understanding of the things of God.

This book is a must for every pastor, and Sunday school teacher, and evangelist, for your ministry. This is a spiritual tool that will be a valuable asset to help equip you for the calling has given you to teach the word of God.

Sincerely,
Dr. W. O'Farrell Osborne

It is very evident not only many hours but great passion to help new converts were poured into this much needed work.

Billy Fields

How refreshing it was to read the book! There has been a real void in the church for great discipleship material. The greatest thing about the study book is it would be impossible for the reader to complete without staying in their Bible. Thank you so much for allowing God to help you to meet such an urgent need of training new converts. I know it will serve to bless so many who hunger and thirst for a more detailed look at their Christian faith.

Dr. Calvin Ray Evans
Rubyville Community Church, Pastor
Evangelistic Outreach Ministries, Director

Eagles Nest Ministry

Dr. Todd Br. Zike

629 S. Broadway St.

Blanchester, OH 45107

513-785-9945

The Teacherts Book

This Bible Believer's Basic Bible study book is written with love for my Saviour. With over twenty-five years in the ministry and pastoring four churches, I see such a need for maturity in the Christians' life.

This book along with its teacher books can be used in small groups, family studies, adult Sunday school classes and/or Sunday or Wednesday evening church services. It starts out with your basics and builds a base for young Christians. Also, by rehearsing it with your older Christians, it is geared to fan the flames and to stir their love for Christ. My goal is to see young Christians witnessing and testifying the love of Christ while being faithful in God's house, using both their tithes and talents to serve God.

Many thanks to my wife Diane and my three children, Christy, Chelsea and Caitlyn for their love and devotion to Jesus Christ. I would also like to thank my family for their understanding for the last three months while I spent many family hours in my study working on this book. This is why I would like to dedicate this first book to them.

Thanks also to my Pastor of my youth, Brother Clyde Perry, for his devotion and knowledge of the Word of God and many other pastors and evangelists who have mentored me along life's way. A big thanks also to Sue Glassmeyer for typing and helping set up this book.

My prayer is that this book will ground each and every young Christian in the faith helping them to be a productive part of the family of God.

This Book: The Bible Believers'
Basic Bible Study
can also be used as a student's
book to go along with
The Book: Teacher copy of
The Bible Believers'
Basic Bible Study
For more information, call
1-513-785-9945

A Tribute to the Bible

God's Word is the traveler's map, the pilot's compass,
the soldier's sword and the believer's log.

The Bible contains light to direct you, comfort to console you, food to sustain you,
wisdom to teach you and fire to warm you.

This Book reveals the mind of God, the original state of man,
the way of salvation and the doom of sinners.

Its author is God, its writers were men and its infallibly inspired.

It's given to you in life, opened in judgment, and will endure forever.

It's a mine of wealth, a river of pleasure, and a paradise of glory.

God's glory is its end, the Lord Jesus Christ is its wonderful object,
and our good is its design.

Here heaven opens, paradise is restored, hell's gates are disclosed.

Its history is true, its doctrines are holy, and its precepts binding.

Read it thoughtfully, read it frequently, and read it prayerfully.

Read it to be wise, believe it to be safe, practice it to be holy, memorize it to grow.

It involves the highest responsibility, it will reward the greatest labor and
it will condemn all who trifle with its sacred contents.

Contents

SOURCE

To take you back to where the thoughts of this book began, I must go back to my Calvary experience.

On February 12, 1979, on a Monday night in a family Bible study, I gave my heart to Jesus, asking Him to forgive me of my sins and to come into my life. Immediately my life changed. I called my girlfriend and my friends telling them what had happened to me. I thought everyone would want to do the same thing. My girlfriend, who is now my wife, gave her heart to Jesus along with one of my friends.

I soon found out that not everyone wanted to change; many even seemed to take offence to this man named Jesus.

I found I had a burning desire to learn more about Him. I began reading my Bible every day and going to church whenever the doors were opened. It all seemed so natural to me. I began going out on visitation, inviting others to come to church, asking people if they were saved. If they said no, I would give them the plan of salvation and ask them to accept Jesus into their hearts.

Many of the people who said they were saved didn't even go to church, or they couldn't remember the name of their church or their pastor's name. This always haunted me how someone can claim to be a Christian and never go to the house of God or read His Word.

Then, on October 17, 1983, on a Monday night in a revival service in Norwood, Ohio I surrendered my call to preach. I began by having such a burning desire for God's Word and for lost souls. The call to preach was like my conviction when I was lost, it's something hard to explain but something you know. That following Sunday, I announced my call at Fellowship Tabernacle in Cincinnati, Ohio. Pastor Clyde Perry was the pastor of whom I owe a debt of gratitude, for all the love and knowledge which he has imparted to me. I spent seven years under Pastor Perry and three years under Pastor Huesman, during which time we started a church from scratch in Mason, OH.

I kept watching people quit or drop out of church for petty reasons and sometimes for no reason at all. I was then an intern pastor for <u>one</u> year and then I pastored a Baptist church in Hamilton, Ohio for <u>one</u> year.

It seemed so easy for me when I got saved, no one really told me what to do, I just figured if you loved Him you would want to learn more about Him by reading the Bible and praise Him in His house.

I then moved to Selinsgrove, Pennsylvania and took a small church, The Sound of the Gospel, where I pastored for <u>ten</u> years. It started out with around 40-50 people, but God immediately began to bless the church by saving souls. We soon out grew our 150 seat church building and started a building program. We soon had a new sanctuary which could seat up to 500 people.

People began to talk about the building not being brick, the former pastor wanting to change the name of the church, (and the list goes on and on and on). I saw good people leave, young Christians drop out, and a cell group in the church leave to start another church. When all this was happening my heart seemed to break in two and I experienced more pain than any physical injury could cause. But in the valley of pain, God began to speak to me about discipleship and a great need to anchor young Christians. I have been teaching bits and pieces of this book for the last couple of years but have decided to put it together in an easy to study outline chapter form. I hope this book helps your family, friends and your church to be established in the faith. I believe if you take young Christians and run them through the eight lesson program it will anchor them in their faith.

This program is designed to take a young Christian from milk and in 3 months having them drink water and having them go on to meat.

(I Peter 2:2) *"As newborn babes, desire the sincere milk of the Word, that ye may grow thereby."*

As a young Christian, we should have a desire to read and look into the Word of God. The apostle Paul, when he was writing to Corinth rebuked the people, telling them they should be ashamed for not growing and that the cause of all their strife and division is because they are still carnal babes in Christ.

(I Corinthians 3:1-3) *"And I, brethren, could not speak unto you as unto spiritual, but as unto carnal, even as unto babes in Christ. I have fed you with milk, and not with meat: for hitherto ye were not able to bear it, neither yet now are ye able. For ye are yet carnal: for whereas there is among you envying, and strife, and divisions, are ye not carnal, and walk as men?"*

These are the verses that God brought to my heart in the middle of strife and division. Paul was saying when I left you that you were young babes in Christ and you needed milk, then Paul says when I came back to you, you were still young babes in Christ crying for milk.

The time frame between Paul's visits was approximately three to three and a half years. Paul was telling them in three to three and a half years you should grow from <u>a carnal babe in Christ</u> to a <u>spiritual adult in Christ</u>.

But we see the evidence of them still being babes in Christ:

1. <u>Envying</u>
2. <u>Strife</u>
3. <u>Divisions</u>

We can see this in our churches today. This is what prompted me to write a book of the basic simple doctrines and beliefs that need to be instilled in every young believer's life. I thought hard about not putting our church's problems in this book. Usually we glamorize and want people only to see, hear or read about the good things in our life, but it was in the deepest pain that God gave birth to this book for me. <u>Out of pain came forth pleasure.</u>

It is a pleasure for me to see young Christians dig into this study and grow into spiritual adulthood. May God bless and anoint this book as it is intended to build His kingdom.

Straight
From the
Bible

WHAT YOU SHOULD KNOW

PROBLEM ~ SIN

"For all have sinned, and come short of the glory of God." (Romans 3:23)

PENALTY ~ SEPARATION (DEATH)

"For the wages of sin is death." (Romans 6:23)

"And death and hell were cast into the lake of fire. This is the second death." (Revelation 20:14)

PROVISION ~ SUBSTITUTION (DELIVERER)

"But God commendeth His love toward us, in that, while we were yet sinners, Christ died for us." (Romans 5:8)

PROMISE ~ SALVATION

"For whosoever shall call upon the name of the Lord shall be saved." (Romans 10:13)

PRAYER ~ SUPPLICATION (CALL)

Dear Lord, I realize I am a lost sinner. Please forgive my sins. I now by faith alone receive you, Jesus, as my personal Saviour. Thank you, Lord, for saving me as you promised. Amen.

PROGRESS ~ SANCTUARY (CHURCH)

"Not forsaking the assembling of ourselves together, as the manner of some is." (Hebrews 10:25)

PURPOSE ~ SERVICE

"For we are His workmanship, created in Christ Jesus unto good works, which God hath before ordained that we should walk in them." (Ephesians 2:10)

Chapter I

SALVATION

The Father wrought it, the Son bought it, the Spirit taught it, the devil fought it, the rich man sought it, the dying thief caught it, and thank God I've got it - salvation.

To become a saint we must first realize we are a sinner.

A. The Way To Salvation

(Romans 3:10) *"As it is written, There is none righteous, no, not one."*

(Romans 3:23) *"For all have sinned, and come short of the glory of God."*

First: We must realize the world and all the people therein have become guilty before God. We are all sinners and therefore we all deserve judgment and death. Adam and Eve, when they were created, had great fellowship with God. God put them in the garden of Eden to dress it and keep it.

(Genesis 2:16-17) *"And the Lord God commanded the man, saying, Of every tree of the garden thou mayest freely eat:"* (17) *"But of the tree of the knowledge of good and evil, thou shalt not eat of it: for in the day that thou eatest thereof thou shalt surely die."*

Adam and Eve, though created by God, He gave them a free will of choice. Of course we see where man falls in (Genesis 3:6-7) *"And when the woman saw that the tree was good for food, and that it was pleasant to the eyes, and a tree to be desired to make one wise, she took of the fruit thereof, and did eat, and gave also unto her husband with her; and he did eat."* (7) *"And the eyes of them both were opened, and they knew that they were naked; and they sewed fig leaves together, and made themselves aprons."*

God told them the day they ate of the tree, they would surely what? die

The day they ate of the fruit <u>spiritual death</u> was immediate for their eyes were opened, then they hid themselves from God.

Before they had great <u>fellowship</u>, now they are in <u>hiding</u>.

Before, they could have physically lived <u>forever</u>. Now not only does spiritual death take place immediately, but <u>physical death</u> now is eminent.

The first thing Adam and Eve do is try to cover exposed sin by sewing fig leaves together and cover their sin by <u>works</u>.

The first thing God does is shed the blood of the animals and cover their sin by the <u>blood</u>.

(Genesis 3:21) ***"Unto Adam also and to his wife did the Lord God make coats of skins, and clothed them."***

Then confirming the blood as the early covering and sacrifice we have (Genesis 4) where Cain rises up and slays his brother Abel.

Why did Cain kill his brother Abel?

<u>He was jealous of his brother's sacrifice being accepted by God and not his.</u>

Abel sacrificed the firstling of his flock = <u>blood</u>

Cain offered the fruit of the ground = <u>works</u>

(Genesis 4:4-5) ***"...and the Lord had respect unto Abel and to his offering:"*** (5) ***"but unto Cain and to his offering He had not respect."***

It takes blood to cover sin; man's work and righteousness are nothing more than filthy rags. Abel's blood cried out from the ground to God (Genesis 4:10). God hears and sees the blood.

Then we see the O.T. law how they were commanded to sacrifice doves, pigeons, bulls, goats, and lambs. Even once a year the High Priest would offer a sacrifice for the nation of Israel and their sin.

Today we are born into sin because of the fall of Adam. We must realize we are a sinner and that we need to be saved. The way of salvation is through the <u>blood</u>.

The Bible says: We can enter into the holiest by the blood of Jesus.

(Hebrews 9:22) *"And almost all things are by the law purged with blood; and without shedding of blood is no remission."*

(Acts 20:28) We see Paul's charge to the elders.
"Take heed therefore unto yourselves, and to all the flock, over the which the Holy Ghost hath made you overseers, to feed the church of God, which He hath purchased with His own blood."

It's God's church and He paid for it with His own blood. It's the Father's blood that the child carries which courses through their veins.

If God is the Father, and Jesus is the Son, whose blood coursed through Jesus veins?
God's

Remember Mary was a virgin when she was found with child of the Holy Ghost.
It's very important to know that it was not mortal blood shed at Calvary, but it was immortal blood of God shed at Calvary.

That's why in the O.T. the blood covered sins.
Then in the N.T. Jesus' blood cleanses sins.

There is only one sacrifice that needs to be applied; there is only one road through salvation. The way of salvation is through the blood.

B. The Who Of Salvation

(Acts 4:10-12) *"Be it known unto you all, and to all the people of Israel, that by the name of Jesus Christ of Nazareth, whom ye crucified, whom God raised from the dead..."* (12) *"Neither is there salvation in any other: for there is none other name under heaven given among men, whereby we must be saved."*

(John 14:6) *"Jesus saith unto him, I am the way, the truth, and the life: no man cometh unto the Father, but by me."*
Jesus lets His disciples know that the only person that we can go to and get to the Father is through Himself. **"There is no other."**

We know: A) The way of salvation: <u>Blood</u>

B) The who of salvation: <u>Jesus</u>

(I John 1:7) ***"...and the blood of Jesus Christ His Son cleanseth us from all sin."***

C. **The Words Of Salvation**

In just a moment we will look at the vocabulary of salvation but first here are a few good verses to help lead someone to Christ.

(Romans 10:9-13) ***"That if thou shalt confess with thy mouth the Lord Jesus, and shalt believe in thine heart that God hath raised Him from the dead, thou shalt be saved."*** (10) ***"For with the heart man believeth unto righteousness; and with the mouth confession is made unto salvation."*** (11) ***"For the scripture saith, Whosoever believeth on Him shall not be ashamed."*** (12) ***"For there is no difference between the Jew and the Greek: for the same Lord over all is rich unto all that call upon Him."*** (13) ***"For whosoever shall call upon the name of the Lord shall be saved."***

(John 3:3) Jesus speaking to Nicodemus

"Jesus answered and said unto him, Verily, verily, I say unto thee, except a man be born again, he cannot see the kingdom of God."

We need to be <u>saved</u>, <u>born again</u>, and <u>converted</u> by acknowledging our sin, asking forgiveness and believing that He (Jesus Christ) is able to deliver us. It's more than just repeating a prayer; it is Godly sorrow of our sins and faith in Jesus.

(II Corinthians 7:10) ***"For Godly sorrow worketh repentance to salvation..."***

(Romans 6:23) ***"For the wages of sin is death; but the gift of God is eternal life through Jesus Christ our Lord."***

Q. Do you know that you are saved? <u>Yes</u>

Q. How? <u>Word of God</u>

The Bible says in (Ephesians 2:8-9) ***"For by grace are ye saved through faith; and that not of yourselves: it is the gift of God:*** (9) ***"Not of works, lest any man should boast."***

Some are still trying to get in by the way of works. It didn't work for Adam or Cain nor will it work for you and me.

(Titus 3:5) ***"Not by works of righteousness which we have done, but according to His mercy He saved us..."***

We need to take a look at a few words:

    1. <u>Gift of God</u> (John 3:16) ***"For God so loved the world, that He gave His only begotten Son, that whosoever believeth in Him should not perish, but have everlasting life."***

The Gift of God – Is His Son – Jesus.

    2. <u>Grace</u> = Undeserved acceptance and love received from another, especially the characteristic attitude of God in providing salvation to sinners.

(Titus 2:11) ***"For the grace of God that bringeth salvation hath appeared to all men."***

    The gift of God is His Son; the grace of God is the Son giving His life for us.

    3. <u>Faith</u> = Belief and trust in God; complete trust; loyalty.

(Hebrews 11:1) ***"Now faith is the substance of things hoped for, the evidence of things not seen."***

Without faith, we cannot be saved. Without faith, there is no hope for our soul. Without faith, we cannot please God.

(Hebrews 11:6) ***"But without faith it is impossible to please Him: for he that cometh to God must believe that He is, and that He is a rewarder of them that diligently seek Him."***

To summarize we can say

The way of salvation = <u>blood</u>

The who of salvation = <u>Jesus</u>

The words of salvation = <u>gift,</u> <u>grace</u>, and <u>faith</u>.

Now once you and I have come the way of the blood and ask in Godly sorrow for Jesus to forgive us of our sins and to come into our life by faith, what takes place?

    We are * <u>Forgiven of our sins</u>

        * <u>Flooding of peace in our soul</u>

        * <u>Filling of the Holy Spirit</u>

Once conviction has taken place and we ask in Godly sorrow for forgiveness of sin and we ask Jesus to save us, then the Holy Spirit takes up residence in our lives. This is what changes us and gives us a whole new outlook on life.

(II Corinthians 5:17) *"Therefore if any man be in Christ, he is a new creature: old things are passed away; behold, all things are become new."*

Remember Jesus said when He left that He would not leave us comfortless.

(John 14:16) Jesus says *"I will pray the Father, and He shall give you another Comforter, that He may abide with you for ever."* (VS 26) *"But the Comforter, which is the Holy Ghost…"*

(I Peter 4:6) *"…, but live according to God in the spirit."*
(Romans 8:9) *"But ye are not in the flesh, but in the Spirit, if so be that the Spirit of God dwell in you."*

The Trinity Verse (Ephesians 2:18) *"For through Him we both have access by one Spirit unto the Father."*

1. Through Jesus
2. Access by Holy Spirit
3. Unto the Father

The Holy Spirit
Always remember He is a real person, the third part of the trinity of God.

When you think of the Bible, break it up into three dispensations.
1. O.T. = The dispensation of God.
2. Gospels = The dispensation of Jesus.
3. N.T. (Rest) = The dispensation of the Holy Spirit.

Don't let someone tell you that the Holy Spirit is a power or a force or that you need to pray so you can receive all the Holy Spirit. He cannot be broken up in pieces; He is a real person and has traits of a real person.

* The Personality of the Holy Spirit:

1. He has a mind (Romans 8:27)

2. He has a will (I Corinthians 12:11)

3. He forbids (Acts 16:6-7)

4. He permits (Acts 16:10)

5. He speaks (Acts 8:29)

6. He loves (Romans 15:30)

7. He grieves (Ephesians 4:30)

8. He prays (Romans 8:26)

** The Emblems of the Holy Spirit:

1. Dove (John 1:32)

2. Water (Isaiah 44:3)

3. Oil (Luke 4:18)

4. Seal (Ephesians 1:13)

5. Wind (John 3:8)

6. Fire (Exodus 3:2)

7. Cloud (Exodus 13:21)

8. Dew (Psalms 133:3)

*** The Titles and Names of the Holy Spirit:

1. The spirit of God (I Corinthians 3:16)

2. The spirit of Christ (Romans 8:9)

3. The spirit of life (Romans 8:2)

4. The spirit of truth (John 16:13)

5. The spirit of grace (Hebrews 10:29)

6. The spirit of glory (I Peter 4:14)

7. The spirit of promise (Acts 1:4-5)

8. The spirit of adoption (Romans 8:15)

9. The spirit of holiness (Romans 1:4)

10. The spirit of faith (II Corinthians 4:13)

* The eternal spirit, the spirit of wisdom and revelation, the Holy Ghost, the Holy Spirit and the Comforter.

**** The Deity of the Holy Spirit:

1. He is omnipresent (Psalms 139:7)

2. He is omniscient (I Corinthians 2:10-11)

3. He is omnipotent (Genesis 1:2)

4. He is eternal (Hebrews 9:14)

5. He is called God (Acts 5:3-4)

6. He is made equal with the Father and Son (Matthew 3:16-17; 4:1-7; John 14:16, 26)

The Holy Spirit right now acts as a divine dam, holding back and limiting the full power of Satan and sin. One day soon God will remove this divine dam and all those who possess Him will be exempt and then judgment and war, killing, pestilence and sin will break forth like never before. So we are all sinners who need a Saviour. God loved us so much He gave us a gift. Jesus came to earth and died on Calvary and shed His blood. Because of God's grace and mercy we can accept this gift and receive the promise of the Holy Spirit to live in our lives. We believe that Jesus arose out of the tomb on that third day and therefore we have victory in Him.

If you have been born once - you must die twice.

But if you have been born twice - you only have to die once.

The Vocabulary of Salvation

A. Remission

B. Redemption

C. Regeneration

D. Reconciliation

E. Origination

F. Supplication

G. Sanctification

H. Substitution

I. Preservation

J. Propitiation

K. Adoption

L. Conversion

M. Imputation

N. Justification

O. Glorification

1. __Conversion (L)__ = Turn from sin to God, a sincere change in the mind of a sinner, causing him to turn from his sin.

(Psalms 19:7; Psalms 51:3, Matthew 18:3; Acts 3:19; 15:3; James 5:20)

2. __Substitution (H)__ = Act of one person, standing instead of another person.

(I Peter 3:18; Genesis 22:10-13; Exodus 12:3-7; 12-13)

3. __Reconciliation (D)__ = Hebrew word Kaphar = To cover something.

Greek word Allasso = Change from that of enmity to that of friendship.

(II Corinthians 5:19; Matthew 5:24; Romans 5:10-11; 11:15; I Corinthians 7:11; Ephesians 2:16; Colossians 1:20-22)

4. __Propitiation (J)__ = To render favorable, to satisfy, to appease.

(I John 2:2; 4:10; Romans 3:25)

5. __Remission (A)__ = To erase or to remit.

(Acts 10:43; Matthew 26:28; Luke 24:47; Hebrews 9:22)

6. __Redemption (B)__ = Threefold meaning to ransom, remove, and release.

(Luke 1:68; Galatians 3:13; Revelations 5:9; O.T. The Kinsman Redeemer)

7. __Regeneration (C)__ = Second birth (John 3:3).

(Titus 3:5; Matthew 19:28)

8. __Imputation (M)__ = To add to one's account.

(James 2:23; Romans 4:22-23; Romans 4:11)

9. __Adoption (K)__ = Giving Christians the position of the children of God.

(Galatians 4:4-5; Romans 8:15, 23; Ephesians 1:5)

10. __Supplication (F)__ = Earnest prayer (having fellowship with God).

(Ephesians 6:18; I Timothy 2:1; Philippians 4:6)

11. __Justification (N)__ = Old timers said it meant "Just as if I never had sinned".

(Romans 5:l, 16, 18; Job 25:4; Romans 4:25)

12. Sanctification (G)   = To be set apart (1,060 times found in the Bible).

(Leviticus 11:44; Ephesians 5:25-26; I Thessalonians 4:3; 5:23; John 17:19)

13. Glorification (O)   = The ultimate physical, mental, and spiritual perfection of believers.

(Romans 8:30; Romans 5:2; I Corinthians 15:43; Colossians 3:4; I Peter 1:5)

14. Preservation (I)   = Keeping power.

(I Thessalonians 5:23-24; Jude l)

15. Origination (E)   = Decree, ordain, foreknowledge, election, council, predestination, purposed and called, initiate, begin.

(Colossians 1:16; Revelation 4:11)

The gospel is written a chapter a day, by the deeds that you do, and the words that you say. The world reads what you say, whether faithless or true. (say) What is the gospel according to you?

SALVATION: God set up a temporary covering in the O.T. law through the sacrificing of animals and the shedding of their blood. It took faith in the O.T. to believe that the death and blood of an animal would cover their sins. Then we have the one time sacrifice of Jesus in the N.T. Those that come to Him by faith receive the cleansing of sin. After accepting God's gift and His grace and mercy we now are saved. The Holy Spirit sets up residence in the Christian's life.

Remember:

• God never intended for man to die.

Through the choosing of the freewill of man (Adam) we chose to die, spiritually and physically. (I Corinthians 15:22) *"For as in Adam all die, even so in Christ shall all be made alive."*

• God never created Hell for man.

Once again through the freewill of man and his choice, many men choose hell today. God does not send man to hell, but rather man chooses to go there himself.

(II Peter and Jude) *"And the angels which kept not their first estate, but left their own habitation, He hath reserved in everlasting chains under darkness unto the judgment of the great day."*

- God is still giving men and women choices today.

- God loves all mankind and wishes no one to perish.

- God can only save someone when conviction is present.

- God wants all mankind to repent and be saved.

Jesus said: **"Repent for the kingdom of heaven is at hand."**

Paul said: **"Command all men everywhere to repent."**

Peter said: **"Repent and be baptized everyone."**

John the Baptist said: **"I baptize you with water unto repentance."**

Twelve Apostles said: **"They went out and preached that men should repent."**

Q. Have you repented of your sins? Yes   Are you saved? Yes

Salvation: A. Ask   E. Everlasting Life

   B. Believe   F. Faith

   C. Confess   G. Grace

   D. Delivered   H. Heaven will be our home

The Assurance Of Our Salvation

(I John 5:13) *"These things have I written unto you that believe on the name of the Son of God; that ye may know that ye have eternal life, and that ye may believe on the name of the Son of God."*

We have the Word of God to verify and establish salvation in our heart. We can know that we know that we know that we are saved and born again by the grace of God. Amen.

ASSURANCE OF SALVATION TEST

1. According to this verse (John 3:17), why did God send His Son into the world?
   "…that the world through Him might be saved."

2. According to (John 3:18), people are divided into two groups, name these groups.
   A. Not condemned   B. Condemned

3. What prompted God to send His Son into the world? (John 3:16)
   God so loved the world

4. What is promised to those who believe on God's Son? (John 3:16)
   Everlasting life

5. According to this verse (Titus 3:5), it was God's what that saved us?
   Mercy

6. According to this verse (Ephesians 2:8), we are saved by something and through something.   A. By: Grace   B. Through: Faith

7. How can we know that we have passed from death unto life? (I John 3:14)
   "Because we love the brethren."

8. Since God promised everlasting life to those who believe on the Son, then why do some still have a feeling of condemnation after their conversion? (Romans 8:1)
   "Because they're walking after the flesh."

9. What is the change in a person after he is saved? (II Corinthians 5:17)
   "Old things are passed away; behold all things are become new."

10. What are some old things – and – what are some new things?
    Old life, old man, old self, old sin.
    New life, new man, new self, new start with my sins removed. (Praise God!)

11. Who is the one who lives in you since you are saved? (John 14:16) And is He a real person? (Ephesians 2:18)
    The Comforter / The Holy Spirit / Yes, He is the 3rd part of the Trinity.

12. Are you sure, beyond any shadow of a doubt, about your salvation? Yes

13. If you should doubt your salvation, what should you do? (I John 5:13; Romans 10:17)
    You should believe on God's Word.
    Read God's Word – and increase your faith.

Someone once said to be a good salesman one must know and believe in their product. I believe to be a good witness and soul winner one must first know Jesus, then must be sure about their salvation.

Salvation: (Noah Webster 1828)

1. The act of saving; preservation from destruction, danger or great calamity.

2. Appropriately in theology, the redemption of man from the bondage of sin and liability to eternal death, and the conferring on him everlasting happiness. This is the great Salvation. Godly sorrow worketh repentance to salvation. 2 Corinthians VII.

3. Deliverance from enemies; victory. Exodus XIV

4. Remission of sins, or saving graces. Luke XIX

5. The author of man's salvation. Psalms XXVII

6. A term of praise or benediction. Revelations XIX

How can I know I am saved?

* Did you repent of your sins? <u>Yes</u>

* Did you ask Jesus to come into your heart? <u>Yes</u>

If you could not answer these both 'yes', you first need to do both of these things.

Then we can know that:

    1. God promised us eternal life- God does not lie.

    2. God's Word has it recorded - God's Word will never pass away.

    3. Our name is written in the Lamb's Book of Life.

Because of these things we should rejoice in our salvation, and have security in knowing that we are saved. I believe we should know that we know that we know that we are saved! Once we nail this down in our Christian walk, we can be a great witness and soul winner for Jesus Christ.

What a change He has made in my life and I pray He has made a change in yours also.

The Bible says that from the beginning God has chosen you and me to salvation. (II Thessalonians 2:13)

My closing remark and question comes from the scriptures and is found in (Hebrews 2:3). *"How shall we escape, if we neglect so great salvation…"*

For more references on salvation in the N.T. see:

(Matthew 9:13; 18:11; Mark 2:17; Luke 1:77; 2:30; 3:6; 13:5; 19:9; John 3:3; 15-18; 4:22; 6:35, 48-58; 8:12, 36; 9:5; 10:10; Acts 2:38; 4:12; 13:26, 47; 16:17; 28:28; Romans 1:16; 10:9-13; 11:11; 13:11; II Corinthians 6:2; 7:10; Ephesians 1:13; Philippians 2:12; I Thessalonians 5:8-9; II Thessalonians 2:13; II Timothy 3:15; Titus 2:11; Hebrews 1:14; 5:9; I Peter 1:5, 9-10; Jude 3; Revelations 19:1…)

Chapter II

<u>SANCTUARY</u>

<u>Sanctuary:</u> (Noah Webster 1828)

A sacred place; particularly among the Israelites, the most retired part of the temple at Jerusalem, called the Holy of Holies, in which was kept the ark of the covenant, and into which no person was permitted to enter except the High Priest, and that only once a year to intercede for the people. The same name was given to the most sacred part of the Tabernacle. Lev. IV, Heb. IX

2. The Temple at Jerusalem 2 Chron. XX

3. A house consecrated to the worship of God; a place where divine service is performed. Ps lXXIII Hence <u>Sanctuary is used for a church.</u>

4. In Catholic churches, that part of the church where the altar is placed, encompassed with a balustrade.

5. A place of protection; a sacred asylum. Hence a Sanctuary-man is one that resorts to a Sanctuary for protection.

6. Shelter; protection.

<u>Church:</u>

1. A house consecrated to the worship of God; the Lord's house...

2. The collective body of Christians, or of those who profess to believe in Christ, and acknowledge Him to be the Saviour of mankind...

<u>The meaning of the word "church"</u>

The Greek word in the New Testament for our English word church is <u>Ekklesia</u>.

It is derived from the word <u>Ekkaleo.</u>

 <u>Ek</u> = Out

 <u>Kaleo</u> = To call or summon

Therefore the literal meaning of church is to: <u>call out</u>.

I think we as a church have been called out of the world to be separated, different and one day we will be called out to spend eternity with our Lord.

A) **<u>Sanctuary of the Body</u>**

Jesus when talking about His body said:

* <u>The Saviour</u> (Matthew 26:61) ***"...I am able to destroy the temple of God, and to build it in three days."***

(Mark 14:58) ***"We heard Him say, I will destroy this temple that is made with hands, and within three days I will build another made without hands."***

These words were taken from Jesus after He had purged the temple driving out those who sold oxen, sheep and doves making money in the house of God.

The Jews then ask Jesus for a sign to prove that it was proper for Him to do these things.

(John 2:19-21) ***"Jesus answered and said unto them, destroy this temple, and in three days I will raise it up."***

(20) ***"Then said the Jews, Forty and six years was this temple in building, and wilt thou rear it up in three days?"***

(21) ***"But He spake of the temple of his body."***

What temple was Jesus talking about tearing down? <u>The building</u>

What temple was Jesus talking about raising up? <u>His body</u>

The O.T. represented the <u>Law</u>

The N.T. represents <u>Grace</u>

(John 12:32) Jesus said:

"And I, if I be lifted up from the earth, will draw all men unto me."

Jesus was lifted up and shed His blood at Calvary and on that third day He rose victorious over death, hell and the grave. Now because He lives today you and I can also live not only now, but for all eternity.

28

In the Old Testament the <u>blood</u> was brought into the sanctuary.

(Hebrews 13:11) *"For the bodies of those beasts, whose blood is brought into the sanctuary by the high priest for sin, are burned without the camp."*

Think of it!!! The Old Testament we see: * <u>The Beast</u> (Animal)

* <u>The Blood</u> (Animals' Blood)

* <u>The Bringing</u> (Carrying)

* <u>The Bearer</u> (High Priest)

* <u>The Blanket</u> (For Sin)

In the New Testament we see some changing going on.

* <u>The bodies of the beast"</u>   Becomes the body of Christ

* <u>"Whose blood is brought into the sanctuary"</u>   God brought His blood (Acts 20:28) into the sanctuary of Jesus His Son.

* <u>"By the high priest"</u>   Jesus Christ is the high priest who offered His blood in the temple on Calvary.

* <u>"For sin"</u>   No longer a blanket to cover but a blood that banishes and cleanses sin. This is the mystery of snow.

(Job 38:22) *"Hast thou entered into the treasures of the snow?..."*

Every single snow flake is formed around a particle of dirt and dust called a speck. This can only be seen through a microscope. So beautiful on the outside, but inside so small we can not see it, but it's dirty.

(Psalm 51:7) *"Purge me with hyssop, and I shall be clean: wash me, and I shall be whiter than snow."*

When Jesus washes you and I through the blood He doesn't cover sin anymore, He takes it out. (Praise God!) We become whiter than snow, because Jesus' blood removes the speck.

<u>Self</u> (I Corinthians 6:19) *"What? know ye not that your body is the temple of the Holy Ghost which is in you, which ye have of God, and ye are not your own?"*

(I Corinthians 3:16-17) *"Know ye not that ye are the temple of God, and that the Spirit of God dwelleth in you?"* (17) *"If any man defile the temple of God, him shall God destroy; for the temple of God is holy, which temple ye are."*

We were created in the image of God; therefore our bodies are the temple of God. The Spirit of God (Holy Ghost) is to dwell in us, and we are to walk in the spirit so we don't fulfill the lusts of the flesh. If we defiled the temple of God then we reap judgment upon ourselves.

O God, help us to understand we were created a holy temple to praise you.

(II Corinthians 6:16-18) *"And what agreement hath the temple of God with idols? for ye are the temple of the living God; as God hath said, I will dwell in them, and walk in them; and I will be their God, and they shall be my people."* (17) *"Wherefore come out from among them, and be ye separate, saith the Lord, and touch not the unclean thing; and I will receive you."* (18) *"And will be a Father unto you, and ye shall be my sons and daughters, saith the Lord Almighty."*

* God wants to live in us and move in us through the presence of the Holy Spirit.
* God wants us to: separate and come out from among them.
* God wants us to: separate ourselves from unclean things.

God wants to be our Father.

God wants us to be sons and daughters.

We have looked at the sanctuary of the body of

* Saviour
* Self

B) **Sanctuary of the Brethren**

* Saints (Matthew 16:18) Jesus said, *"And I say also unto thee, That thou art Peter, and upon this rock I will build my church; and the gates of hell shall not prevail against it."*

Jesus is not telling Peter to build a church and call it St. Peter's Rock of Jesus Christ Church.

Jesus is telling Peter, that upon this rock, <u>Jesus</u> being this rock, that I (Jesus) will build my (Jesus) church. This church will not be stationary but will be on the offensive. The gates of hell are stationary; we are to attack the gates of hell with the keys of the kingdom, thus building the church.

(Matthew 16:19) *"And I will give unto thee the keys of the kingdom of heaven: and whatsoever thou shalt bind on earth shall be bound in heaven: and whatsoever thou shalt loose on earth shall be loosed in heaven."*

These keys to the kingdom are given to everyone who knows Christ as their Saviour. We have the scriptures and the interpretation thereof through the Holy Spirit.

If we withhold the Word of God we <u>bind</u> it.

If we give out the Word we <u>loose</u> it.

We, <u>the body of believers</u>, are the church of God.

(Acts 2:47) *"… and the Lord added to the church daily such as should be saved."*

God did not come down and keep building a material church of wood or stone, God added to the body of believers in Christ which is the <u>church</u>.

The Bible says:

<u>Saul</u> "made havoc of the church."

<u>Paul</u> "feed the church of God."

(Ephesians 5:25-27) *"…Christ also loved the church, and gave Himself for it;"*

(26) *"That He might sanctify and cleanse it with the washing of water by the word,"*

(27) *"That He might present it to Himself a glorious church, not having spot, or wrinkle, or any such thing; but that it should be holy and without blemish."*

All these scriptures along with many others showed the church as not being a building, but rather a body of believers. The church, the blood washed, the redeemed.

We are now going to take a look at the symbols of the church.

* <u>Symbols</u>

1. **<u>The Head and the Body</u>** (Romans 12:4) *"For as we have many members in one body…"* (I Corinthians 6:15; 12:12, 13, 27; Ephesians 4:4; 5:30…)

2. **The Bridegroom and the Bride** (II Corinthians 11:2) *"For I am jealous over you with Godly jealousy: for I have espoused you to one husband, that I may present you as a chaste virgin to Christ."* (Revelation 21:9; Ephesians 5:14-27)

3. **The Vine and the Branches** (John 15:1-5) *"I am the true vine, and my Father is the husbandman."* (2) *"Every branch in me that beareth not fruit He taketh away…"* (Judges 9:7-15; Psalm 80:8; Isaiah 5:1-7; Ezekiel 15:2; Hosea 10:1)

4. **The Shepherd and the Sheep** (John 10:11) *"I am the good shepherd: the good shepherd giveth His life for the sheep."* (Hebrews 13:20; I Peter 5:4; Psalm 23)

Jesus is our Shepherd, Good Shepherd, Great Shepherd, and Chief Shepherd.

5. **The High Priest and a Kingdom of Priests** (I Peter 2:9) *"But ye are a chosen generation, a royal priesthood…"* (Revelation 1:6; 5:10; 20:6)

Old Testament Priest ~ offered up sacrifices.

New Testament Priest ~ should offer up sacrifices.

A) Our Person (Romans 12:1)

B) Our Praise (I Peter 2:5, 9)

C) Our Provisions (Hebrews 13:6)

6. **The Corner Stone and the Living Stones** (Ephesians 2:19-22) *"…Jesus Christ Himself being the chief corner stone…"* (I Peter 2:4-5)

One day God will touch Jesus on the shoulder and tell Him to go get his children. Then Christ shall rise and come to get the church (the invisible body of believers) and bring us home. He knows each and every one; they all have the same blood type. What a day that will be!

This is the Bride of Christ, the Lamb's Wife, the church.

C) **Sanctuary of the Building**

Sanctuary, building, church, temple, structure, a place that is dedicated to praise and worship God in.

First we see the garden where Adam and Eve had fellowship with God.

(Genesis 2:8) *"And the Lord God planted a garden eastward in Eden; and there He put the man whom He had formed."*

Then when sin had entered the heart of man, God banished them from the garden.

Second we see a general place where Cain and Abel brought their sacrifices.
(Genesis 4:3-4) *"...Cain brought of the fruit..." "And Abel, he also brought of the firstlings of his flock..."*
They both brought their sacrifice for God to a certain location. In the beginning God sacrifice the blood of animals for Adam and Eve. Abel's blood sacrifice was accepted but Cain's work sacrifice was not. (The place was thought to be the entrance of the garden.)
Third we see Noah after the flood, sacrifices a burnt offering to God at Mount Ararat.
Fourth we see Abraham (Genesis 22) taken to a certain place Mount Moriah to offer up his son Isaac; instead a ram was offered in his place.
Fifth we see the nation Israel delivered from the Egyptians by the blood of the lamb.
(The Passover Exodus 12) the death angel only claimed those without the blood.
"When I see the blood I will pass over you."
Sixth we see Moses now at Mount Sinai receiving instruction from God to build an altar and a sanctuary to offer sacrifices in.

- He was to sprinkle the blood on the altar
- He was to read the Word of God
- He was to sprinkle the blood on the people
- He was given the Ten Commandments
- He was to build a sanctuary for God

(Exodus 25:8) *"And let them make me a sanctuary; that I may dwell among them."*
God now commands a certain place built solely for worship, sacrifice and praise for Him.
(Exodus 25:9) *"According to all that I shew thee, after the pattern of the tabernacle..."*
1) Tabernacle found some 344 times in the Word of God. This word means tent of meeting a sacred tent, a portable and provisional sanctuary, where God met His people. The court was formed by curtains attached to erect poles, always erected to face the East. This was a certain place designated to worship God. Within there lies the golden altar, laver of brass, the Holy place and the most Holy place called the Holy of Holies (The place where God dwells). He can only be approached with the blood.

2) <u>Temple</u> found some 224 times in the Word of God. A place of worship, a sacred or holy place called temple, meaning house of God. (Temple of Solomon built in Jerusalem) David, a Godly man and King but a man of war, was not permitted to build the temple, so he began to gather the material for Solomon his son. (A man of great wisdom) This temple was dedicated to be used as the house of God. A permanent dwelling place inside ten layers of brass, five on each side of the temple, the molten sea (lower center) and the altar of burnt offerings (center), of course then the porch, the Holy place and the Holy of Holies.

3) <u>Synagogue</u> found some 68 times in the Word of God. The synagogue had its roots in the time after Solomon's temple was destroyed and many of the people were carried into exile. Local worship and instruction became necessary. Even after many of the Jews returned to Jerusalem and rebuilt the temple, places of local worship continued. By the time of Jesus visits these places and assemblies were called synagogues…

Most communities of any size had at least one synagogue; some had several…

The principal meeting was on the Sabbath (Saturday).

Jesus customarily went to the synagogue in His hometown of Nazareth.

(Luke 4:16) ***"And He came to Nazareth, where He had been brought up: and, as His custom was, He went into the synagogue on the Sabbath day, and stood up for to read."***

Once Jesus begins His public ministry, He frequently taught, preached, and healed in the synagogues throughout the land.

(Matthew 4:23; 9:35; Mark 1:39; Luke 4:31-37, 44)

So we see in the Old Testament worship started in the <u>garden</u> then went to a <u>general place</u> where Cain and Abel offered sacrifices.

Then we see Noah on <u>Mount Ararat</u> offer a sacrifice to God.

Then comes Abraham who offered a ram on <u>Mount Moriah</u>.

Then the Passover for the nation of Israel so they can leave the bondage of Egypt.

Then we come to Moses who receives instructions from God on <u>Mount Sinai</u>.

We then see the building of the <u>tabernacle</u> which brings us to a permanent place called the <u>temple</u>.

We then go to many permanent places of worship called the <u>synagogue</u>.

This leads us into the New Testament where we see people who believe this Jesus Christ is the Messiah, the Son of God.

These Jews and early believers assembled themselves together in the upper room in <u>a</u> <u>house</u>.

They met for a short time in houses until they could build <u>churches</u>.

They used to worship on the main Sabbath (Saturday).

Today we worship Jesus on the Lord's Day (Sunday).

(Matthew 28:1) ***"In the <u>end of the Sabbath</u>, as it began to dawn toward the <u>first day of</u>*** ***<u>the week</u>, came Mary Magdalene and the other Mary to see the sepulchre."***

(Mark 16:1) ***"And when the <u>Sabbath was past</u>, Mary Magdalene, and Mary the mother*** ***of James, and Salome, had bought sweet spices, that they might come and anoint*** ***Him."***

* (Luke 24:1) ***"Now upon the <u>first day of the week</u>, very early in the morning, they*** ***came unto the sepulchre, bringing the spices which they had prepared, and certain*** ***others with them."***

The Bible of course goes on to say that the

A) Stone was rolled back

B) Sepulcher was empty

C) Saviour had risen

(Luke 24:5-6) ***"...Why seek ye the living among the dead?"***

"He is not here, but is risen:..."

Today most Christians worship Jesus Christ on Sunday.

<u>Saturday</u> = <u>Sabbath</u> (Law)

<u>Sunday</u> = <u>Lord's Day</u> (Grace)

Let's look at a worship service in the Word of God.

Now Mary Magdalene has come to tell the disciples that she has seen the Lord.

(John 20:19) ***"Then the same day at evening, being the first day of the week, when the doors were shut where the disciples were assembled for fear of the Jews, came Jesus and stood in the midst, and saith unto them, Peace be unto you."***

Here we are on a Sunday night and all the disciples except for Thomas are assembled in the room with the door shut. (This is a meeting or assembly, this is church.)

I preach a message on this text called:

"The man who missed the Sunday night service."

A) He missed sweet fellowship   (VS 19)   "the disciples were assembled"

B) He missed seeing Jesus   (VS 19)   "came Jesus and stood in the midst"

C) He missed the splendor of the resurrected body   (VS 20)   "He shewed unto them"

D) He missed the spectacular joy and gladness   (VS 20)   "Then were the disciples glad"

E) He missed the great sayings of the good commission   (VS 21)   "send I you."

F) He missed the breathing on of the Holy Spirit of God   (VS 22)   "He breathed on them"

G) He missed the strong transferring of power   (VS 23) "Whose soever sins ye remit, they are remitted…whose soever sins ye retain, they are retained."

H) He missed having his sure faith built up   (VS 25)   "We have seen the Lord."

I) He missed Sunday night service   (VS 24)   "But Thomas, one of the twelve, called Didymus, was not with them when Jesus came."

(John 20:26) ***"And after eight days again His disciples were within, and Thomas with them: then came Jesus, the doors being shut, and stood in the midst, and said, Peace be unto you."***

Here we are once again on Sunday with the disciples worshiping Jesus behind closed doors. And this time Thomas is with them, he doesn't miss out the second time on the blessings of God.

If you missed church you miss out on something God has for you that can never be duplicated the exact same way.

- Praise God for the Old Testament law and New Testament grace
- Praise God for the first day of the week
- Praise God for the Lord's Day

- Praise God for Resurrection <u>Day</u>
- Praise God for <u>Sunday</u>

(Colossians 2:16) ***"Let no man therefore judge you in meat, or in drink, or in respect of an holyday, or of the new moon, or of the Sabbath days:"***

There are some who preach that if you don't worship on a certain day you will go to hell. This is not according to the Word of God!

Sunday was good enough for the early church and it's good enough for me. (Praise God!)

4) <u>Church</u> found some 125 times in the Word of God.

Remember the word church is <u>Ekklesia</u> and it is derived from the word <u>Ekkaleo</u>.

<u>Ek</u> = <u>Out</u>

<u>Kaleo</u> = <u>to call or summon</u> Thus literally meaning = <u>to call out</u>.

We already looked at the word church as being the body of believers. Now we are going to take a few minutes and look at the building or structure that houses the body of believers.

God has always used designated places for worship, and He always will.

Have you ever heard:	"It's my only day of rest."	(No time)
	"I can worship God anywhere."	(Fishing, hunting, etc.)
	"I can worship God at home."	(On T.V. – no fellowship)
"You don't need to go to church to worship God."		(Free will – choice)

People that say these things go contrary to the Word of God. Though in some cases people cannot attend church, such as sickness, or the very elderly in rest homes, most of the time it is the free will of man that says 'no' to church. The church should visit the sick and elderly and encourage all others to come to the house of God. In fact, God commands us to go to church.

(Hebrews 10:25) ***"Not forsaking the assembling of ourselves together, as the manner of some is; but exhorting one another: and so much the more, as ye see the day approaching."***

Shouldn't We Love Church?

(Psalm 26:8) *"Lord, I have loved the habitation of thy house, and the place where thine honour dwelleth."*

(Psalm 122:1) David said: *"I was glad when they said unto me, Let us go into the house of the Lord."*

You should love your church, and be excited when it's time for services to begin, knowing Jesus has something to give you new and afresh every time. There are only two kinds of churches today.

1. Church of Our Saviour Those who preach and teach Jesus Christ's death, burial, and resurrection giving salvation invitation to the sinner, and encouragement to the saint.

2. Church of Satan Those who preach and teach any other doctrine. (Revelation 2:9)

* The positions of the church

Saviour Jesus Christ: is the head of the church (Colossians 1:18)

"And He is the head of the body, the church:…"

(Ephesians 1:23; 2:16; 4:12, 16; 5:23; Colossians 3:15)

Shepherd, Pastor, Bishop, Elder: The pastor is considered to be the single elder in the church. He is called and elected by the church, and then falls under the command of the Chief Shepherd Jesus Christ. (I Timothy 3:1-7; Titus 1:5-9…)

(Hebrews 13:17) *"Obey them that have the rule over you, and submit yourselves: for they watch for your souls, as they that must give account, that they may do it with joy, and not with grief: for that is unprofitable for you."*

A true Pastor and shepherd loves his sheep and prays for them in times of trouble. A hireling will flee and leave when trouble comes his way.

Deacons: (I Timothy 3:8-12; Romans 12:7; Philippians 1:1)

Praise God for some good deacons who will support and help the Pastor, and care for the needs of God's people.

* The Places of the Church

1.	The Church in Jerusalem	(Acts 2:41, 47)
2.	The Church in Antioch of Syria	(Acts 11)
3.	The Church in Antioch of Pisidia	(Acts 13)
4.	The Church in Lystra	(Acts 14)
5.	The Church in Derbe	(Acts 14)
6.	The Church in Iconium	(Acts 14)
7.	The Church in Thessalonica	(Acts 17)
8.	The Church in Philippi	(Acts 16; Philippians)
9.	The Church in Berea	(Acts 17)
10.	The Church in Athens	(Acts17)
11.	The Church in Corinth	(Acts 18; Corinthians)
12.	The Church in Ephesus	(Acts 18, 19; Ephesians; Revelation)
13.	The Church in Troas	(Acts 20)
14.	The Church in Rome	(Romans)
15.	The Church in Galatia	(Galatians)
16.	The Church in Colosse	(Colossians)
17.	The Church in Babylon	(I Peter 5)
18.	The Church in Smyrna	(Revelation 2)
19.	The Church in Pergamos	(Revelation 2)
20.	The Church in Thyatira	(Revelation 2)
21.	The Church in Sardis	(Revelation 3)
22.	The Church in Philadelphia	(Revelation 3)
23.	The Church in Laodicea	(Revelation 3)

God sure did establish a church body of believers, but He also established the church buildings. Today people are trying to get away from the name church; they say it offends people and they use the phrase saying, "We want to be people friendly."

Some call it a meeting place, center, tabernacle, hall or some other name and they drop the name church. Listen, Jesus didn't die for a fellowship hall or a center, He died for the church! (Ephesians 5:25)

* <u>The Purpose of the Church</u>

1. <u>It is to love God</u>   (Revelation 2:1) Writing to Ephesus

"Nevertheless I have somewhat against thee, because thou hast left thy first love,"

2. <u>It is to evangelize the world</u>   (Matthew 28:19-20; Mark 16:15; John 20:21; Acts 16)

The Great Commission *"Go ye therefore."* (teach and preach with great power)

3. <u>It is to minister the ordinances</u>   (Matthew 28:19; I Corinthians 11; John 13:5-17)

    A) <u>Baptism</u>   B) <u>Lord's Supper</u>   C) <u>Feet Washing</u>

4. <u>It is to care for its own</u>   (II Corinthians 8:9; I Timothy 5:1-16; James 1:27)

5. <u>It is to come together in fellowship</u>   (Acts 2:42; I Corinthians 1:9; II Corinthians
8:4; 13:14; Galatians 2:9; Philippians 1:5; 2:1; I John 1:6-7)

6. <u>It is to fight the enemy</u>   (Ephesians 5:10-18; Ephesians 6; II Timothy 2)

7. <u>It is to glorify God</u>

    * Through our witnessing   (II Thessalonians 3:1)

    * Through our giving   (Philippians 4:18; Hebrews 13:16)

    * Through our preaching   (I Peter 4:11)

    * Through our praise and prayer   (Hebrews 13:15; John 14:13; Psalm 50:23)

"Whoso offereth praise glorifieth me;…"

Acknowledgment of the Sanctuary Test

1. The literal meaning for the word church is? _____Called out_____

2. Please list at least three symbols of the church. (Ex: Cornerstone and Living Stones)
Head and Body   _Bridegroom and Bride_   _Vine and Branches_   _Shepherd and Sheep_   _High Priest and Kingdom of Priest_

3. According to (Genesis 2) where did Adam and Eve have fellowship with God?
Garden eastward in Eden

4. What mountain did Noah sacrifice to God on? _Mount Ararat_

5. What mountain did Abraham offer Isaac upon? _Mount Moriah_

6. What mountain did Moses received the Ten Commandments on? _Mount Sinai_

7. What was Moses given the pattern for in (Exodus 25:9)? _Tabernacle_

8. What did Solomon build to worship God in? _Temple_

9. When the temple was destroyed what did the Jews build to worship God in?
Synagogue

10. The early believers worshiped in _Houses_ before they could build their _Churches_

11. The Sabbath is mainly what day? _Saturday_ (Law)

    The Lord's Day is what day? _Sunday_ (Grace)

12. What are we commanded to do in (Hebrews 10:25)? _Go to church_

    Name as many of the purposes of the church that we went over in our study.
To love God   _Evangelize the world_   _Minister ordinances_   _Care for its own_   _Come together for fellowship_   _Fight the enemy_   _It is to glorify God_.

Don't Wait for the Hearse to take you to Church

If you wait for the hearse to take you to church:

You will go regardless of the weather.

You will go no matter how your family feels.

You will go regardless of the condition of your body.

You will have beautiful flowers but you will not enjoy them.

Regardless of how good the singing is, you will not enjoy it.

Regardless of what the minister may say, it will do you no good.

You will go to the altar, but you will not pray.

You may have a great need, but no one will be able to help you.

You will never be able to attend church again.

There will be relatives/friends there, but you won't worship together.

You will go regardless whether you're needed at home or on the job.

The minister would rather help you now than try to console

your loved one if you die without God.

Make it your choice to go to church.

Romans 10:17 says: "Faith cometh by hearing, and hearing by the Word of God."

Chapter III

SUPPLICATION

Supplication: (Noah Webster 1828)

1. Entreaty; humble and earnest prayer and worship. In all our supplications to the Father of mercies, let us remember a world lying in ignorance and wickedness.

2. Petition; earnest request

3. In Roman antiquity, a religious solemnity observed in consequence of some military success. It consisted in sacrifice, feasting, offering thanks, and praying for a continuance of success.

Prayer: (Noah Webster 1828)

1. In a general sense, the act of asking for a favor, and particularly with earnestness.

2. In worship, a solemn address to the supreme being, consisting of adoration, or an expression of our sense of God's glorious perfections, confessing our sins, supplication for mercy and forgiveness, intercession for blessings on others, and thanksgiving, or an expression of gratitude to God for His mercies and benefits, a prayer however may consist of a single petition, and it may be extemporaneous, written or printed.

3. A formula of church service, or of worship public or private.

4. Practice of supplication.

5. That part of a memorial or petition to a public body, which specifies the request or thing desired to be done or granted, as distinct from the recital of facts or reasons for the grant. We say the prayer of the petition is that the petitioner may be discharged from arrest.

Q. What is the word that turns back the shadow of death on the face of life's dial?

Q. What is the word that gives us songs in the night?

Q. What is the word that brings angels down from heaven?

Q. What is the word that lifts the load of guilt from the conscience smitten heart?

Q. What is the word that calls the wanderer from the far country?

Q. What is the word that is the best physician for both soul and body?

Q. What is the word that is the simplest form of speech that infant lips can try?

Q. What is the word that is all power and can reach the Majesty on high?

Q. What is the word that makes angels rejoice when they hear it from the lips of sinners?

Q. What is the word that places a hedge around our family and friends?

Q. What is the word that turns captivity captive?

Q. What is the word that is so precious that it's placed into a golden vial?

This word is <u>Prayer</u>

I personally feel that prayer is essential for every born again Christian. Prayer is man's way of talking to God, the same way that the Bible is God's way of talking to man. We should come to Him in praise, thanking Him for what He has done for us and has given to us. We should come to Him reverently with our petitions and requests, knowing always that He knows what is best for each one of us. Prayer is the most effective tool we have in our Christian walk. My aim for this study is to show you the importance and the constant need for prayer. I could give you testimony after testimony on how God answers prayer. But instead we will just get our answers about prayer from the Word of God.

<u>Prayer</u> should be <u>praise</u> and it should be <u>regularly asking</u> God for our needs and <u>yielding</u> to God through our <u>earnest</u> prayer and looking to <u>receive</u> our hearts petition.

"Praise God"

* <u>Mr. D.L. Moody</u> wrote about nine (9) elements of prayer:

1. <u>Adoration</u>	2. <u>Confession</u>	3. <u>Restitution</u>
4. <u>Thanksgiving</u>	5. <u>Forgiveness</u>	6. <u>Unity</u>
7. <u>Faith</u>	8. <u>Petition</u>	9. <u>Submission</u>

Mr. D. L. Moody, Mr. Knox, Mr. Whitefield, Mr. Wesley, Mr. Finney, Mr. Trotter, Mr. Wycliff, Mr. Livingston, Mr. Sunday, and in our day Mr. Evans, Mr. Bowman, Mr. Perry, Mr. Duncan, Mr. Mayfield, Mr. Fields, Mr. Hain, Mr. Witmer, Mr. Graham, Mr. Osborn and thousands and thousands of other great men of faith, became established, equipped, and encouraged through prayer.

Martin Luther said when he was most pressed with work:

"I have so much that I cannot get on without three hours of prayer a day."

Not only was prayer powerful for men in the past but also for women such as:

Corrie Ten Boom, Gladys Aylward, Amy Carmichael, Mary Slessor, Catherine Booth, and in our day Mrs. Depoi, Mrs. Clayborn, Mrs. Fair, Ms. Mitchell, and the list goes on and on and on as I'm sure you could add to these lists of Godly men and women prayer warriors. Thank God for Godly men and women who set aside time daily to reach the throne of God.

In the Bible we see great men and women of God who had great power in prayer such as:

Abraham, Elijah, Paul, Ruth, Esther, Mary, these saints of God along with many others seen great things done through prayer. Even young people such as David and Samuel accomplished much through prayer.

* It does not matter if you are male or   female.
* It does not matter if you are black or   white.
* It does not matter if you are young or   old.
* It does not matter if you are strong or   weak.
* It does not matter if you are short or   tall.
* It does not matter if you are thin or   fat.

If you love God and follow His commandments and pray, God hears your prayers and will answer. You will find favor with God and God will show favor to you. (Praise the Lord!)

A. **The Ways of Prayer**

First we must realize that God will not hear the prayers of a sinner, except the prayer of salvation. A lot of people pray today, who do not even have Jesus as their Savior. He will only hear the prayers of His children or the prayers of someone wanting to become one of His children.

(Acts 10) We meet a man of Caesarea, a Centurion named <u>Cornelius</u>. He is a devout man that feared God and gave alms to the people of God. ***"And prayed to God always."*** Then he sees an angel of the Lord.

(VS 4) ***"…Thy prayers and thine alms are come up for a memorial before God."***

(VS 5) ***"And now send men to Joppa, and call one Simon, whose surname is Peter."***

Now we are going to look at a man named <u>Peter</u>. He is lodging at Simon, a tanner's house in Joppa.

(VS 9) ***"…Peter went up upon the house top to pray about the sixth hour:.."***

Peter goes up to pray at noon upon the house top, while praying he is hungry and he falls into a trance. He sees heaven opened and a great sheet let down, with all manner of four footed beasts, then there comes a voice saying: ***"Rise, Peter; kill and eat."***

Peter says: ***"Not so Lord."*** He had been commanded according to the law not to eat such things. This was done three times then the sheet was taken up into heaven.

Right here I believe the prayer of a sinner <u>Cornelius</u> connects with the prayer of a saint <u>Peter</u>. God was preparing Peter to preach the gospel to the house of Cornelius. Now the men Cornelius has sent are at the door of Simon the tanner. Peter, thinking about this vision, is now told by the Spirit of God that <u>three</u> men seek thee. The Spirit tells him (VS 20) ***"Arise therefore, and get thee down, and go with them, doubting nothing: for I have sent them."***

Peter then goes and tells them about Jesus and they receive the Holy Spirit and are saved.

- God hears the prayer of the sinner for salvation.
- God always uses a vessel to proclaim the gospel.
- God wants you and me to be a willing vessel.

(John 9:31) ***"Now we know that God heareth not sinners: but if any man be a worshipper of God, and doeth His will, him He heareth."***

✝ Here are some prayers for a sinner for salvation. (Romans 10:9-10; John 3)

(VS 9) ***"That if thou shalt confess with thy mouth the Lord Jesus, and shalt believe in thine heart that God hath raised Him from the dead, thou shalt be saved."***

(VS 10) *"For with the heart man believeth unto righteousness; and with the mouth confession is made unto salvation."*

(John 3:3) *"Jesus answered and said unto him, Verily, verily, I say unto thee, Except a man be born again, he cannot see the kingdom of God."*

Jesus loved us in that *"while we were yet sinners, Christ died for us."*

The prayer for salvation does not have to be long for it to be effective.

1) The Publican (Luke 18:13) *"God be merciful to me a sinner."*

2) The Thief (Luke 23:42) *"Lord, remember me when thou comest into thy kingdom."*

Then we remember the great question asked by the keeper of the prison to Paul and Silas.

(Acts 16) Question: *"What must I do to be saved?"*

   Reply: *"Believe on the Lord Jesus Christ, and thou shalt be saved and thy house."*

- So the very first prayer we must pray is the prayer of salvation.

- We must have Godly sorrow.

- We must believe on Jesus Christ as our Saviour.

Prayer started all the way back in Genesis, as Adam talked to God. We then see Abel sacrifices the lamb then God sees the blood and has fellowship with and honors Abel's sacrifice. Cain in anger rises up against his brother, Abel, and slew him.

God starts the next conversation with Cain and asks him: *"Where is Abel thy brother?"*

Then he asks him: *"What hast thou done?"* *"The voice of thy brother's blood crieth unto me from the ground."* Then the curse was placed upon Cain and he was made a fugitive and a vagabond upon the earth.

(Genesis 4:26) *"And to Seth, to him also there was born a son; and he called his name Enos: then began men to call upon the name of the Lord.*

Prayer dates back to the beginning of man and has been an essential part of every Christian believer.

* <u>Pattern of Prayer</u> (Luke 11:1-4; Matthew 6:8-13)

(VS 1) ***"And it came to pass, that, as He was praying in a certain place, when He ceased, one of His disciples said unto Him, Lord, teach us to pray, as John also taught his disciples."***

(VS 2) ***"And He said unto them, When ye pray, say, Our Father which art in heaven, Hallowed be thy name. Thy kingdom come. Thy will be done, as in heaven, so in earth."***

(VS 3) ***"Give us day by day our daily bread."***

(VS 4) ***"And forgive us our sins; for we also forgive every one that is indebted to us. And lead us not into temptation; but deliver us from evil."***

This shows us the importance of prayer. If it was important for His disciples to ask Him to teach them to pray it should be also important to us. If we stay within the bounds of certain general principles of prayer we can learn the following:

1) <u>How to begin</u>   2) <u>Whom to address</u>   3) <u>Whose name to reverence</u>

4) <u>Whose will to obey</u>   5) <u>Whose interest to serve</u>   6) <u>What to ask for</u>

7) <u>How to keep clear channels</u>   8) <u>How to live with fellow man</u>

9) <u>How to live with God</u>   10) <u>How to live free from sin</u>

There is nothing in the Christian life quite as important as prayer.

Prayer is to the <u>spiritual</u> life, like air to the <u>physical</u> life.

The life set and most profitable exercise for the Christian life is prayer.

The disciples realized their need for powerful prayer. The disciples knew how to pray, but they wanted to pray like Jesus with great power.

Like a son or daughter asking their father to teach them how to hit a ball, they want to hit it the correct way like daddy so it will go far.

<u>This prayer is for believers!!!</u> (It is not for the unsaved.)

What are some key things we can learn from the Lord's prayer?

- <u>The ignorance of Prayer</u>   ***"Lord, teach us to pray"***

- <u>The instruction of Prayer</u>   ***"When ye pray, say, Our Father"***

- <u>The imperativeness of Prayer</u>   ***"Thy will be done"***

- <u>The implication of Prayer</u>   ***"Give us day by day our daily bread"***

This is both <u>physical</u> and <u>spiritual</u> bread.

48

- <u>The imprint of Prayer</u>   *"Forgive us" "We forgive everyone"*
- <u>The influence of Prayer</u>   *"Lead us not into temptation"*
- <u>The impact of Prayer</u>   *"But deliver us from evil"*

Let's look at this teaching and pattern for prayer:

✝✝✝✝✝✝✝   <u>IMPORTANT</u>   ✝✝✝✝✝✝✝

I. <u>Prayer is to the Father</u>.   *"When you pray, say Our Father"*

Jesus starts out by telling us who our prayer is addressed to!

(John 15:16) *"…whatsoever ye shall ask of the Father in my name, He may give it you."*

(Matthew 6:6) (Closet Prayer) *"…pray to thy Father which is in secret; and thy Father which seeth in secret shall reward thee openly."*

(James 1:17) *"Every good gift and every perfect gift is from above, and cometh down from the Father…"*   We pray to the Father!

II. <u>Prayer is in the name of the Son</u>.

(John 14:6) Jesus said: *"…I am the way, the truth, and the life: no man cometh unto the Father, but by me."*

(VS 13-14) *"And whatsoever ye shall ask in my name, that will I do, that the Father may be glorified in the Son." "If ye shall ask any thing in my name, I will do it."*

(I John 2:1) *"…And if any man sin, we have an advocate with the Father, Jesus Christ the righteous:"*

* We pray to the Father in the name of the Son!

III. <u>Prayer is in the Holy Spirit</u>.

(Jude 20) *"But ye, beloved, building up yourselves on your most holy faith, praying in the Holy Ghost,"*

(I Corinthians 14:15) *"What is it then? I will pray with the Spirit,…"*

(Galatians 4:6) *"And because ye are sons, God hath sent forth the Spirit of his Son into your hearts, crying, Abba, Father."*

We pray to the <u>Father</u>, in the name of the <u>Son</u>, in the <u>Holy Spirit</u>!

Our address, petition, our prayer is to <u>God the Father</u> in the name of <u>Jesus</u> (through the blood) in agreement with the <u>Holy Ghost</u> who lives inside the believer.

We then make our petition in <u>faith continually</u> knowing He hears and answers our prayers.

IV. <u>Prayer is in Faith</u>.

(Mark 11:24) ***"Therefore I say unto you, What things soever ye desire, when ye pray, believe that ye receive them, and ye shall have them."***

(James 5:15) ***"And the prayer of faith shall save the sick..."***

V. <u>Prayer is in Continuance</u>.

Jesus after healing the man with the withered hand, made enemies; as the enemies increase let us look at and see where Jesus goes to.

(Luke 6:12) ***"...He went out into a mountain to pray, and continued all night in prayer to God."***

After this we see the Beatitudes and the Sermon on the Mount.

(Acts 6:4) The twelve apostles call a multitude of the disciples together and tell them to pick out seven men of honest report full of the Holy Ghost to minister to the widows so they can devote themselves to <u>praying</u> and <u>reading</u>.

These were and are two of the most important things in a dedicated Christian life.

* <u>Places of Prayer</u>

(I Timothy 2:8) ***"I will therefore that men pray everywhere, lifting up holy hands, without wrath and doubting."***

* <u>Bush</u>	(Exodus 3)	Moses
* <u>Garden</u>	(Matthew 26:36)	Jesus
* <u>Cross</u>	(John 19:30)	Jesus
* <u>Cave</u>	(Genesis 32)	Jacob
* <u>Church</u>	(Acts 12)	Church
* <u>Closet</u>	(Matthew 6:6)	You and I
* <u>Hell</u>	(Luke 16:27)	Rich Man

* House	(Daniel 6:10)	Daniel
* House of the Lord	(II Kings 19)	Hezekiah (134 word prayer)
* Jail	(Acts 16:25)	Paul and Silas
* Mount Carmel	(I Kings 18)	Elijah (63 word prayer)
* Mountain	(Matthew 14:23…)	Jesus
* Synagogues	(Matthew 6:5)	Hypocrites
* Temple	(I Samuel 1:9-17, 27)	Hannah
* Wall	(II Kings 20:2)	Hezekiah
* Wilderness	(Numbers 11)	Moses
* Whale	(Jonah 2:1)	Jonah

"Then Jonah prayed unto the Lord his God out of the fish's belly,"

(VS 2) *"…out of the belly of hell cried I, and thou heardest my voice."*

And the list of places continues on and on in the Word of God.

I think this helps us understand that no matter where we are, that we can pray and talk to God. One of the main reasons we come to church is not only to praise and preach but also to pray.

(Matthew 21:13) *"…It is written, My house shall be called the house of prayer;…"*

* Positions of Prayer

Peter - prayed while up to his neck in water.

Daniel - knelt at his window in his house as he talked to God three times a day.

Moses - talked to God with his shoes off his feet, as he stood on Holy ground.

Others - some lay prostrate as they cry to God.

some lay fetal as they cry to God.

some pray standing.

some pray sitting.

some pray while exercising.

some pray while working.

The position of prayer is not as important as the heart of prayer.

(I Timothy 2:8) *"…that men pray everywhere."*

We can pray anywhere and everywhere. What a privilege that God has given us.

May we always and continually talk to our Father.

B. **The Whys of Prayer**

The word prayer is found some <u>583</u> times in the Word of God and supplication is found <u>58</u> times.

Prayer is one of the main topics and subjects in the Word of God. I've dedicated at least 10 messages to the single topic of prayer, and many others with prayer being one of the main ingredients.

1)	<u>Prayer</u>	(Luke 11:1-4)
2)	<u>Ask for a Mountain</u>	(Joshua 14)
3)	<u>The Worst Prayer Ever Offered</u>	(Luke 14:15-24)
4)	<u>Let's Fill Up at the B.P. Station</u>	(I Chronicles 4:9-10)
5)	<u>When 1 + 1 = 3</u>	(Matthew 18:19-20)
6)	<u>What the Church Needs That Hell Has</u>	(Luke 16:19-31)
7)	<u>The Praying Bulldog</u>	(Matthew 26:36-46)
8)	<u>Helping Hands</u>	(Exodus 17:8-14)
9)	<u>Somebody Touched Heaven for Me</u>	(Exodus 17:8-13)
10)	<u>When There Is Nothing</u>	(I Kings 18:41-46)

Let's take a look at some of the reasons why we pray!

* <u>Sinners and Foes</u>

<u>Sinners</u> (Romans 10:1) ***"Brethren, my heart's desire and prayer to God for Israel is, that they might be saved."***

Paul prayed for the sinners. If we could only put a face to some of the people in hell we would pray ***"None perish, no not one."***

Jesus was so broken over sinners, we see Him praying in the garden then we see the prayer and the plea for workers. (Matthew 9:38) ***"Pray ye therefore the Lord of the harvest, that He will send forth labourers into His harvest."***

In (Luke 6:12), Jesus continued all night in prayer to God, and if Jesus saw Israel as lost sheep and would cry and weep over them, shouldn't you and I carry a burden, weep and pray for the lost?

<u>Foes</u> (Matthew 5:44) and in (Luke 6:28) ***"But I say unto you, Love your enemies, bless them that curse you, do good to them that hate you, and pray for them which despitefully use you, and persecute you;"***

* Saints and Family

Saints Paul said on at least five different occasions that he would lift up his brothers and sisters in prayer.

(Romans 1:9) *"...that without ceasing I make mention of you always in my prayers;"*

Jesus was praying for Peter and said in (Luke 22:32), *"But I have prayed for thee, that thy faith fail not: and when thou art converted, strengthen thy brethren."*

Oh God, help us to pray for our brothers and sisters in Christ. Pray for their needs, burdens, and for their spiritual insight and strength.

✝✝✝✝✝✝✝   IMPORTANT   ✝✝✝✝✝✝✝

According to (Galatians 6:2), we should be what? Burden bearers

"Bear ye one another's burdens, and so fulfil the law of Christ."

If someone has a need, we should immediately take that need to God. We should pray with the one that has the need.

In church if someone goes up to pray at the altar, why don't you go with them placing your hand on their back, letting them know they're not alone? It's just nice to know that you have others that will share your burdens.

One burden shared by two equals one half.

* Sickness and Faults

Sickness (James 5:15-16) *"And the prayer of faith shall save the sick..."*

(16) *"Confess your faults one to another, and pray one for another, that ye may be healed. The effectual fervent prayer of a righteous man availeth much."*

Today I believe God works through doctors and hospitals, but I still believe God touches and heals many times just through prayer. (Pray first.)

When it seems like we can find no help or answers with the doctors, may we take our physical needs to the Great Physician.

(Jeremiah 8:22) *"Is there no balm in Gilead; is there no physician there? why then is not the health of the daughter of my people recovered?"*

Again and again and again when Jesus would touch a physical need, He would say, *"Thy faith has made thee whole."* Let us take our physical needs to Him, in faith believing He can and will for His glory heal our sickness. (Praise God!)

<u>Faults</u> (Galatians 6:1) ***"Brethren, if a man be overtaken in a fault, ye which are spiritual, restore such an one in the spirit of meekness; considering thyself, lest thou also be tempted."***

(I John 2:1) ***"My little children, these things write I unto you, that ye sin not. And if any man sin, we have an advocate with the Father, Jesus Christ the righteous:"***

We should pray for our shortcomings, our faults, and if need be our sins once we are saved. Although God has given us provision not to sin (Romans 5:20; Romans 6:1) He has given us an advocate to go to. (Thank you, Lord, for your mercy and grace.)

When talking about the <u>whys of prayer</u>, we talked about some reasons why we pray.

- We are to pray for the <u>sinners</u> and our <u>foes</u>.

- We are to pray for the <u>saints</u> and our <u>family</u>.

- We are to pray for the <u>sickness</u> and our <u>faults</u>.

- We are to pray for: <u>power</u>, <u>praise</u>, <u>protection</u>, <u>promises</u>.

* The theme of this chapter is that Godly men and women <u>pray</u>! When Godly prayer and supplication isn't enough, prayer warriors go down on their knees with a broken heart and an empty stomach. This is when <u>fasting</u> is added to prayer.

<u>Fasting</u> This word is found some 116 times in the Word of God.

(Matthew 17:21) and in (Mark 9:29) ***"Howbeit this kind goeth not out but by prayer and fasting."***

The Lord in (Matthew 10) had sent out His disciples with power against unclean spirits, to cast them out and to heal all manner of sickness and disease.

The Jews religiously fasted. In fact, once it was asked why Jesus' disciples fasted not. We of course know the reason was as stated in Jesus' reply that He, the Messiah, was with them.

Now Jesus sends them out and He stays back to wait for their return. They come back rejoicing but Jesus tells them not to rejoice because of these things but to rejoice because their name is in the book of life.

This is now where we pick up the reading in (Matthew 17:14-21).

We see a man's son possessed, but Jesus' disciples could not deliver him. Jesus then delivers the man's son. When the disciples asked Him why they could not do it, He then replies with ***"...this kind goeth not out but by prayer and fasting."***

Jesus was not with them. That was the time when they were doing work for the kingdom they should have also been fasting.

Today Jesus physically is not with us. In time of trouble, revival, special needs, you and I should pray and fast.

Here are a few other verses that you may want to look into about fasting.

(Matthew 6:16; Matthew 9; Luke 18:12; Acts 14:23; II Corinthians 11:27...)

Here are a couple of books on fasting and prayer you may find useful.

1) Fasting What the Bible Teaches   By: Jerry Falwell

2) Fasting for Spiritual Breakthrough   By: E. L. Towns

3) Classic Sermons on Prayer   By: Warren W. Wiersbe

4) All the Prayers of the Bible   By: Herbert Lockyer

5) All Things Are Possible Through Prayer   By: C. L. Allen

C. **The When of Prayer**

1. Without Ceasing Prayer

(I Thessalonians 5:17) *"Pray without ceasing."*

(Acts 12:5) *"...but prayer was made without ceasing of the church..."*

2. Continuance Prayer

(Luke 6:12) *"...and continued all night in prayer to God."*

(Acts 1:14) *"These all continued with one accord in prayer and supplication..."*

3. Always Prayer

(Ephesians 6:18) *"Praying always with all prayer and supplication..."*

(Philemon 4) *"...making mention of thee always in my prayers,"*

4. Night and Day Prayer

(I Timothy 5:5) *"...continueth in supplications and prayers night and day."*

5. Midnight Prayer

(Acts 16:25) *"And at midnight Paul and Silas prayed..."*

6. Instant Prayer

(Romans 12:12) *"Rejoicing in hope; patient in tribulation; continuing instant in prayer;"*

I think you understand the importance of prayer. We are commanded to pray continually and always, asking Him for our needs, seeking Him with all our hearts, knocking upon the door. The Bible lets us know that we can come boldly before God's throne, and it also lets us know how to ask.

(Matthew 7:7-8) *"Ask, and it shall be given you; seek, and ye shall find; knock, and it shall be opened unto you:"*
(8) *"For every one that asketh receiveth; and he that seeketh findeth; and to him that knocketh it shall be opened."*

A = Ask
S = Seek
K = Knock

We should ask with simplicity
We should seek with intensity
We should knock with persistency

On the topic of prayer and supplication I feel I just touched on the tip of an iceberg. I used mainly New Testament passages. There are some great Old Testament records of some great men and women of the Bible who fasted and prayed such as: David, Samuel, Elijah, and his great 63 word prayer that brought fire down from heaven. Others such as Elisha, Esther, Hezekiah, Ruth, Daniel, Joshua, and the list goes on.
* Before our testing I'll close with this verse.
(Philippians 4:6) *"Be careful for nothing; but in everything by prayer and supplication with thanksgiving let your requests be made known unto God."*

P = Prevailing	(Genesis 32:28)
R = Requesting	(Matthew 7:7)
A = Accepting	(Matthew 21:22)
Y = Yielding	(Luke 22:42)
E = Evangelizing	(Matthew 28:19, 20)
R = Rejoicing	(John 16:24)

ACCEPTANCE OF SUPPLICATION TEST

1. When Martin Luther was so busy, he said he had to at least pray for how many hours before he could begin his day? _____ Three hours _____

2. If you love God and follow His Commandments, then God will hear and answer our what? _____ Prayers _____

3. When we were going over The Ways of Prayer we realized that according to John 9:31 God heareth not whose prayer? _____ The sinner _____

4. The only sinners' prayer that God will ever hear is the prayer of what (Romans 10:9-10)? _____ Salvation _____

5. In the Lord's prayer and in our own prayer we are to address and pray to who? _____ The Father _____

6. If we are to pray to the Father then we should pray in the name of _____ The Son _____ in the power and presence in _____ The Holy Ghost _____ and our prayers should be prayed in what? _____ Faith _____

7. According to (I Timothy 2:8), where are men to pray? _____ Everywhere _____

8. When we went over places of prayer in the Bible, we listed 18 places where men prayed such as Jonah praying from the belly of a whale. Please list six or more places.
___ House of the Lord ___ , ___ Baptizing ___ , ___ Garden ___ , ___ Cross ___ ,
___ Cave ___ , ___ Church ___ , ___ Closet ___ , ___ Hell ___ ,
___ House ___ , ___ Wilderness ___ , ___ Bush ___ , ___ Jail ___ ,
___ Mount Carmel ___ , ___ Mountain ___ , ___ Synagogues ___ , ___ Temple ___ ,
___ Wall ___ .

9. When going over The Whys of Prayer, we talked about the sinner and foes and about the saints and family and the third thing we talked about was our?
_____ Sickness _____ and _____ Faults _____

10. There is a main ingredient we must mix with prayer and supplication when we have a great need or we have a heavy burden that we desire to be met. This ingredient is found 116 times in the word of God? _____ Fasting _____

11. According to (Galatians 6:2), when others are troubled we are to become their what?
_____ Burden bearer _____

12. When going over <u>The When of Prayer</u>, we listed at least six times of prayer. For example: Without ceasing prayer. Please list as many of the other five as you can.

<u>   Continuance Prayer   </u>, <u>   Always Prayer   </u>, <u>   Night and Day   </u>, <u>   Midnight Prayer   </u>, <u>   Instant Prayer   </u>

* We should A = <u>   Ask   </u> S = <u>   Seek   </u> K = <u>   Knock   </u>

Chapter IV

SCRIPTURES

Scriptures: (Noah Webster 1828)

    1. In its primary sense, a writing; anything written.

    2. Appropriately, and by law of distinction, the books of the old and new Testament; the Bible. The word is used either in singular or plural number, to denote the sacred writings or divine oracles, called sacred or holy, as proceeding from God and containing sacred doctrines and precepts.

There is not any action that a man ought to do or forbear, but the Scripture will give him a clear precept or prohibition for it.   South.

Compared with the knowledge which the scriptures contain, every other subject of human inquiry is vanity and emptiness.   Buckminister.

Bible: (Noah Webster 1828) Greek word meaning The Book

By way of eminence; the sacred volume, in which are contained the Revelations of God, the principles of Christian faith, and the rules of practice.

It consists of two parts, called the old and new testaments.

The Bible should be the standard of language as well as faith.   Anon.

The <u>Holy Bible</u>
Given by a <u>Holy God</u>
Written by <u>Holy Men</u>
Under the power of the <u>Holy Ghost</u>
To be lived by a <u>Holy People</u>

The Bible is written a chapter a day, by the deeds that you do and the words that you say. The Bible you preach whether faithless or true, say what is the Bible according to you?

The reading of the scriptures is essential for every born again Christian. While <u>prayer</u> is man's way of talking to God, the <u>Scriptures</u> are God's way of talking to man. There is nothing as important in a Christian's life as <u>praying</u>, and <u>reading</u> the <u>Word of God</u>. Within its pages lies the power to transform a <u>sinner</u> into a <u>saint</u>, to turn <u>burdens</u> into <u>blessings</u> and to change one's destiny from <u>hell</u> to <u>heaven</u>. My prayer is that you will have an intense desire to read God's Word daily.

The word: <u>Scriptures</u> is found <u>55</u> times in the Bible.

<u>Law</u> is found <u>560</u> times in the Bible.

<u>The Word of God</u> is found <u>199</u> times in the Bible.

<u>Commandments</u> is found <u>341</u> times in the Bible.

<u>Statutes</u> is found <u>166</u> times in the Bible.

<u>Judgments</u> is found <u>127</u> times in the Bible.

There are also many other references to the Bible found in the Word of God, given under different names.

<u>D. L. Moody</u> when almost at the edge of death called for his family to get the Book. Mr. Moody had hundreds and thousands of books, so the normal reply was: *"Which book would you like?"* His reply was: *"There is only one book to die by!"*

How true this statement is, there is only one book to die by, but it's also the book to live by.

Before we start on the background of the Scriptures, there are a couple questions we must ask ourselves.

1. Is the Word of God true? <u>Yes</u>

Is it <u>Firm or Fable</u> ~ <u>Fact or Fiction</u>

    <u>Fixed or False</u> ~ <u>Final or Finite</u>

    <u>Forever or Fairytale</u> ~ <u>Foreordained or Forged</u>?

2. If you believe some of it is true, then how do you pick out what is false?

3. Do you believe it is God's book or is it just a good book?

4. Do you believe it is a Holy book or just a book?

The answers to these questions are very important. Many Christian colleges have changed their statement of faith by adding something at the end.

They used to read something like this:

We believe in the inspired, inerrant and infallible Word of God.

Now they put a tag on the end of their statement that goes something like this:

We believe in the inspired, inerrant and infallible Word of God in its original language.

They are saying that they believe the Holy Spirit led the men to write the original, but they believe that in the translation into the English language that the Holy Spirit wasn't present to preserve His Word.

* The Word of God says in (Psalm 11:3) ***"If the foundations be destroyed, what can the righteous do?"*** * (Psalms 12:6-7) ***"The words of the Lord are pure words: as silver tried in a furnace of earth, purified seven times."***

"Thou shalt keep them, O Lord, thou shalt preserve them from this generation forever."

Can God preserve His word forever? <u>Yes</u>

Can God preserve His word in Greek, Hebrew, Latin, and English? <u>Yes</u>

Are even small details important to God? <u>Yes</u>

* (Matthew 5:18) ***"For verily I say unto you, Till heaven and earth pass, one jot or one tittle shall in no wise pass from the law, till all be fulfilled."*** (From the dotting of the i's to the crossing of the t's)

* (I Peter 1:25) ***"But the word of the Lord endureth forever. And this is the word which by the gospel is preached unto you."***

Today there is a line drawn in the sand over the version of the Bible that we read. The majority of people believed in the multiple versions and that any one will do. The minority believe that the K.J.V. 1611 is the Bible that God inspired in our English language.

✝ I guess the question is now that you and I are saved and born again, which Bible should you read?

Dr. Arthur T. Pierson says: *"...it is remarkable how faithful all the standard translations are...not one affects a single vital doctrine of the Word of God."*

Dr. Robert L. Thomas says: *"And no major doctrine of Scripture is affected by a variant reading."*

Dr. H. S. Miller says: *"No doctrine is affected and very often not even the translation is affected."*

(Dr. Philip Scaff, Dr. Louis T. Talbot, James R. White, and others) All these seem to agree that any English version is OK to read and to set your doctrine and life by.

On the minority side of those that believe that the K.J.V. 1611 is God's inspired, inerrant, and infallible Word of God are (Dr. D. A. Waite, Dr. Peter S. Ruckman, Dr. Roy Branson, Dr. Jack Hyles, Professor G. A. Riplinger, William P. Grady, Dr. Todd Br. Zike and others.)

A. The Background of the Scriptures
* History of the Manuscripts

I still believe (Matthew 24:35) ***"Heaven and earth shall pass away, but my words shall not pass away."***

The Apostle Paul knew men would be corrupting God's Word.

(II Corinthians 2:17) ***"For we are not as many, which corrupt the word of God: but as of sincerity, but as of God, in the sight of God speak we in Christ."***

The Apostle Peter also sounded the warning in (II Peter 2:1-3) ***"But there were false prophets also among the people, even as there shall be false teachers among you, who privily shall bring in damnable heresies, even denying the Lord that bought them, and bring upon themselves swift destruction."***

(VS 2) *"And many shall follow their pernicious ways: by reason of whom the way of truth shall be evil spoken of."* (K.J.V. 1611 Attack)

(VS 3) *"And through covetousness shall they with feigned words make merchandise of you: whose judgment now of a long time lingereth not, and their damnation slumbereth not."*

Peter hits the nail on the head when he says this will be done through covetousness. The number one reason for all these new versions is the greed of money.

The Apostle John when he was on the island of Patmos writes to us with the strongest of all warnings to leave God's word alone.

(Revelation 22:18-19) *"For I testify unto every man that heareth the words of the prophecy of this book, If any man shall add unto these things, God shall add unto him the plagues that are written in this book:"*

"And if any man shall take away from the words of the book of this prophecy, God shall take away his part out of the book of life, and out of the holy city, and from the things which are written in this book."

Scriptures at that time were in the hands of true believers, who copied them with great fear and trembling.

At this time <u>Rome</u> was in power and their form of worship was a combination of Babylonian and Egyptian Paganism.

* <u>Nero</u> the emperor thought himself to be divine and to have reached god status.

* Christians refused to bow to him, thus came the open slaughter of true believing Christians. (Stake, fire, lions, dungeons...)

* In <u>Egypt</u> they decided they would take their god in by communion or eating a sun shaped wafer with the letters <u>I. H. S.</u> which stands for their three Egyptian gods, <u>Isis</u>, <u>Horis</u> and <u>Seth</u>.

* <u>Constintine</u> was a son of an emperor and when his father died he wanted the throne, but he was not in Rome at the time. As the commander of an army he assembled his forces at the Stone Milvian Bridge of the Tiber River on October 28, 312 A.D.

(His enemy was Max Assences.)

* <u>Constintine</u> wanted to win this battle showing his strength so he could rule Rome.

On the way, Constintine has a vision. He sees a cross in the sky and it said to him, *"In this sign conquer."* So he took this cross and painted it on his shields. This cross today we know as an Ankh which is a cross with a circle on top.

After a great victory and slaughter he then proclaimed himself and all his troops as Christians, baptizing his whole troop. Many believe he was the first Christian emperor but history bears out a different story.

Constintine took on the title as the first Pope. (Sumis Pontifis) and in 313 A.D. issued the Edict of Malone called the decree of tolerance which stated Christians were not to be killed anymore. This sounds great, but this is where Constintine now wants to mix Baal worship with Christianity. There are two places where manuscripts are being made.

1) Antioch here we see the true believers making exact copies of God's Word with great fear. The Bible says: ***"They were first called Christians at Antioch."***

2) Alexandria (Egypt) here is where you see a man by the name of Clement and his star pupil whose name is Origen.

(A lot of people think Origen was a great father of the church.)

* First Origen thought Jesus was a lessor deity, he did not think Jesus was God. So when he would come across a manuscript of Jesus Christ, being God, he would cut it up.

* Second Clement and Origen set up Seminary school of Philosophy and higher learning. They thought of themselves as being divine. Therefore as being divine they changed the Word of God by taking away and adding to certain parts and calling it original manuscripts. They thought those men in Antioch to be feeble because they were not able to change the scriptures, with superior knowledge.

* Now Constintine says to Usebeus, I want 50 Bibles made up since now I am a Christian. Usebeus under the rule of Constintine chooses Alexandria to get the Bibles copied, because he too considered Jesus a lesser deity than God.

* Next we see a man called Saint Jerome known to be a Catholic scholar. He took Usebeus' work from Alexandria and made what is called the Latin Vulgate.

This was completed around 480 A.D. Now from 400 to 420 A.D. the question was being asked, *"Which Bible?"*

The Catholic Church is in power and the Latin Vulgate is what they are using.

Now came extreme pressure upon the Christians at Antioch and the hopes to destroy the Antioch Manuscripts.

Now with the Catholic Church in power, they felt only the clergy, priest or Pope could understand God's Word and therefore it should not be given unto the average person (because of their inabilities to understand it).

These Catholic leaders were called Nicolaitanes. This is someone who reads God's Word and says God has given me special understanding, and that His Word is for private or secret interpretation. God hates the Nicolaitanes (Revelation 2).

* Leo I became history's first authentic true Pope by having forcefully secured universal submission to his personal authority.

For the next ten centuries, using the Latin Vulgate, anyone who would not submit would be met with persecution and death. Christians were forced to go underground and thus broke out what we know as the "Dark Ages".

(Hosea 4:6) *"My people are destroyed for lack of knowledge."*

The deplorable conditions continued with the Clergies' suppression of the Scriptures. This came by the council of Toulouse in 1229 A.D. sustaining ignorance of the laity.

This now leads us into the era of the early 1600s and we see King James who has a strong desire to translate the Word of God into English.

There have been a lot of critics write a lot of negative things about King James VI of Scotland and the I of England. He was a God-fearing man and he wanted to get God's Word into the hands of the people.

Some try to say that he was a homosexual monarch. This is taken from his writings in his work Basilicon Doron that: *"There are some horrible crimes that ye are bound in conscience never to forgive: such as witchcraft, willful murder, incest, and sodomy."*

For more details on his life and writings, read:

King James the VI of Scotland & the I of England Unjustly Accused.

Introduced by: His Grace The 10th Duke of Atholl

Written by: Stephen A. Coston Sr.

* __The Holiness of the Men__

King James assembled some 57 scholars together with the command to take the Word of God and translate it word for word into the English language.

They were not allowed to change any word but only to translate. Where it was needed for clarity they would italicize their words. To deviate from this command meant death.

This of course was taken from the Antioch copies of the manuscripts. This text is called the texus receptus.

Six companies of men were drawn for specific work with all six companies at the end checking each other's work. This began in 1604 and ended in 1611 a seven year job with which some died in the process.

There were 47 men at the time of completion. They rejected anything from Alexandria as being corrupt. These men were some of the greatest men whom God had prepared for the accomplishment of this work.

I will list just one or two things about some of these men.

* John Bois At the age of five years old had read the Bible through in Hebrew.

* William Bedwell His fame for Arabic learning was so great that scholars from around the world sought him out for assistance.

* Miles Smith He was an expert in Chaldee (which is related to Hebrew), the Syriac and the Arabic, were as familiar to him as the native tongue.

* Edward Lively One of the best linguists in the world. He was the King's Professor of Hebrew at Cambridge University.

* John Harmen One of the giants of his day, he was the King's Professor in Greek.

One of these men read the Bible 200 times on his knees. I would venture to say very few men and modern translators could ever equal up to any of these men.

1. The superiority of translators themselves.

2. The superiority of the Antioch Manuscripts called the texus receptus.

3. The superiority of the product The Book ~ The King James Bible.

✝ The King James Bible is a word for word translation. Almost all other translations are paraphrased.

This means they try and keep the theme but they put it in their own words.

When they do refer to the manuscripts they refer to those of <u>Alexandria Egypt</u> which they call the older manuscripts (= corrupted manuscripts).

They also slant the Word of God with hidden agendas of their own doctrine and beliefs. Many panel translators today do little to no work on the translation. They are mainly signing for endorsement in which they get money and the company uses their name to promote their version in that denomination or popularity in which they are known.

* <u>The R.S.V.</u> Take a look at just a couple of men on their panel such as R. C. Briggs who openly denies the blood atonement, Dr. Harold Tribble who openly denies the virgin birth, Dr. T. O. Hall who says that the Bible is not the Word of God, Eric Rust who says the Bible is made up of myths. And others, some of which are members of communist organizations, and the list goes on.

* <u>The N.K.J.V.</u> Even their logo is an ancient symbol for the pagan trinity, not the Christian trinity. The symbol was popularized again by satanist High Priest Alister Crowley. Also used on the 3rd degree of the York Order of Masonry. This symbol can be seen on satanic rock group albums like Led Zeppelin and others.

The N.K.J.V. omits words like:

<u>Lord</u>	66 times	<u>Repent</u>	44 times
<u>God</u>	51 times	<u>Blood</u>	23 times
<u>Heaven</u>	50 times	<u>Hell</u>	22 times

The N.K.J.V. was supposed to take out the old Gothic style words and make it easier to understand. I think we all understand words like Lord, God, blood...

This is a selling feature which all new versions use to help promote and sell their product.

* <u>The N.I.V.</u> removes 63,625 words! Once again we hear that it is written to make it easier to understand. Let's look at some of these words that are omitted:

<u>Christ</u>	26 times	<u>Blood</u>	41 times
<u>Lord</u>	352 times	<u>Salvation</u>	42 times
<u>God</u>	468 times	<u>Hell</u>	40 times

Here are some of the complete verses that are taken away!

(Matthew 17:21; 18:11; Mark 7:16; 9:46; 11:26; 15:28; Mark 16:9-20; Luke 17:36;

23:17; 23:17; John 5:4; 7:53; 8:11; Acts 15:34; 8:37; 24:7; 28:29; Romans 16:24 and others.)

(Isaiah 14:12) K.J.V. *"How art thou fallen from heaven, O Lucifer, son of the morning! how art thou cut down to the ground, which didst weaken the nations!"*
(Isaiah 14:12) N.I.V. *"How art thou fallen from heaven, 0 morning star, son of the dawn! you have been cast down to the earth, you who once laid low on nations!"*
(Look at Revelation 22:16)

In the K.J.V. it talks about Lucifer (Satan) son of the morning cast out of heaven, and thrown down to earth, waging war.
In the N.I.V. it talks about the morning star (Jesus) who is cast out of heaven, and thrown down to earth, waging war.

Something is Wrong!

(II Peter 1:21) K.J.V. *"For the prophecy came not in old time by the will of man: but holy men of God spake as they were moved by the Holy Ghost."*
(II Peter 1:21) N.I.V. *"For prophecy never had its origin in the human will, but prophets, though human, spoke from God as they were carried along by the Holy Spirit."*

(I Peter 1:25) K.J.V. *"But the word of the Lord endureth forever. And this is the word which by the gospel is preached unto you"*.
Endureth = literally means there is a battle or opposition
Is = a present term (meaning now)
(I Peter 1:25) N.I.V. *"but the word of the Lord stands forever. And this is the word that was preached to you."*
Stands = gives no thought of struggles or a battle
Was = past (because today they don't believe we have the Word of God.)

(Colossians 1:14) K.J.V. *"In whom we have redemption through His blood, even the forgiveness of sins:"*
The blood is one of the strongest doctrines held by every born again Christian.

(Colossians 1:14) N.I.V. *"in whom we have redemption, the forgiveness of sins."*

Something is Missing!

I have only scratched the surface on some of the differences found in other versions. If I were to go into some details on the differences, we would be reading a four or five volume study.

The N.I.V. is an ongoing trans-denominational effort by more than a hundred top Bible scholars.

One of these is Virginia Mollenkott from William Patterson College. She says (Episcopal The Witness June 1991) *"My lesbianism has always been a part of me."*

Her pro-homosexual book, Is the Homosexual My Neighbor?, echoes her N.I.V. assertion that the Bible censures only criminal offences like "prostitution" and "violent gang rape", not "sincere homosexuals...drawn to someone of the same sex."

Thus we have the changing of the K.J.V. in (I Corinthians 6:9) "effeminate" to the N.I.V. "male prostitute nor homosexual offenders".

Also see other verses: (Deuteronomy 23:17; I Kings 15:12; 22:46; II Kings 23:7...)

Virginia Mollenkott promotes goddess worship.

Quote from Paul English PC (USA) says Mollenkott claimed that Jesus' death was the ultimate child abuse, and a model for human child abuse. "I can no longer worship in a theological context that depicts God as an abusive parent and Jesus as the obedient, trusting child." she declared.

Something is Wrong!

The allowable maximum usable without permission from copyright holders is 200 words. The question may be who owns the N.I.V.? The answer is Zondervan!

And Rupert Murdock owns Zondervan, along with 20th Century Fox, Fox Television, TV Guide, owner and producer of Bart Simpson...He owns the printing rights to the N.I.V. He is called by Mike Royko, a Chicago Tribune columnist, The Prince of Darkness.

Doesn't this make you happy that the K.J.V. has no copyright? It can be duplicated word for word by anybody. (Praise God!)

*A lot of K.J.V. 1611 critics attack its spelling and say there were hundreds of errors. But at this time in history there was no standardized spelling, each scholar spelled the English word the way he heard it. You may have one word being spelled three different ways with each one of them being right. It wasn't until later in its revisions when standardized spelling came into effect when these words were all spelled one way.

A lot of K.J.V. critics say it's hard to read and understand.

It was written in old English and old English is written in part for memorization. Probably if you quote Scripture at all it's from the K.J.V.

When you put the new versions and the King James Version to the Flesh-Kincaid grade level formula, you will discover the following:

The K.J.V. = 5th grade reading level

The N.K.J.V. = 6th grade reading level

The A.S.V. = 6th grade reading level

The G.N.F.M.M. = 7th grade reading level

The N.I.V. = 8th grade reading level

Don't be deceived by the new versions appeal for simplicity, this is a sales pitch to get you to buy these products.

The K.J.V. has ninety-five percent of its words that are one or two syllable Anglo-Saxon words.

Since the K.J.V. has laid claim to these first, the derivative copyright works must replace them with harder, Latinized words which always have three or four syllables: many have suffixes and prefixes.

Just to list a few example changes

K.J.V.	**Reference**	**N.I.V.**
joint	Ephesians 4:16	supporting ligament
told	II Chronicles 2:2	conscripted
image	Hebrews 1:3	representation
called	Hebrews 5:10	designated
old	Hebrews 8:13	obsolete

K.J.V.	Reference	N.K.J.V.
house	II Corinthians 5:2	habitation
give	Ecclesiastes 2:3	gratify
smell	Amos 5:21	savor
little river	Ezekiel 31:4	rivulets
no effect	Galatians 5:4	estranged

According to copyright law, new Bible versions can only be copyrighted as "derivative works". Words must be changed whether they need to be changed or not. And copyright is what it's all about, because without that they make no money.

Today you can choose from hundreds of versions of the Bible. The question is does it matter which one you choose? Yes

Great men of the past used the K.J.V. 1611 such as Spurgeon, Cartwright, Sunday, Wesley, Moody, Livingston, Hudson, even men such as Lincoln and others that were great spiritual and military leaders. The results were revivals in England and America, local churches built and souls being saved. It said that under D. L. Moody's ministry over 1,000,000 were saved.

Today we live in moral decay, we gather in churches for social gatherings, but where are the revivals of the past? I believe there has been a great impact on true revival by the watering down of God's Holy and true word.

I believe that the K.J.V. Bible is God's Holy Word in the English language and that it is the inspired, inerrant, and infallible Word of God.
There are many you can choose from, but to me there is only one.

Q. Can someone get saved from another version? Yes
Just as a song that has Scripture in it can move a person's heart, so can a version of the Bible. To me, man is sin sick and needs to be treated.
To treat sin we have the medicine of the K.J.V.
I believe all other medicines are generic or watered down, why settle for second best!

* <u>Happiness of the Maker</u>

God is happy that we have His Word, and He wants us to tell others. He ordained the twelve and sent them out to preach, but He has also commanded you and me to do the same. Jesus came into Galilee preaching the gospel.

(I Corinthians 1:21) ***"...it pleased God by the foolishness of preaching to save them that believe."***

(Romans 10:8) ***"But what saith it? The word is nigh thee, even in thy mouth, and in thy heart: that is, the word of faith, which we preach;"*** (Romans 10:9-13)

(VS 17) ***"So then faith cometh by hearing, and hearing by the word of God."***

* The word of God is all important and powerful!

(Hebrews 4:2) ***"For unto us was the gospel preached, as well as unto them: but the word preached did not profit them, not being mixed with faith in them that heard it."***

(II Timothy 3:16) ***"All scripture is given by inspiration of God...***

God is happy when we believe in the death, burial, and resurrection of Jesus Christ, and we believe that God is all powerful and can preserve His Word and give it to us, so we can read it and give it to others.

B. <u>The Basics of the Scriptures</u>

There are a total of <u>39</u> Old Testament books.

There are a total of <u>27</u> New Testament books.

Total of Old and New Testament books equal <u>66</u>.

The first <u>five</u> books are called the <u>Pentateuch</u>.

In the Greek this means five, and a book of composition.

We also call these books: <u>the books of Moses</u>, <u>the books of the law</u>, and <u>the books of the covenant</u>.

The books that make up the Pentateuch are:

l) <u>Genesis</u>　　2) <u>Exodus</u>　　3) <u>Leviticus</u>　　4) <u>Numbers</u>　　5) <u>Deuteronomy</u>

The next section in the Old Testament makes up <u>twelve</u> books and these books are called the books of <u>Past History</u>.

    1) <u>Joshua</u>   2) <u>Judges</u>   3) <u>Ruth</u>   4) <u>I Samuel</u>

    5) <u>II Samuel</u>   6) <u>I Kings</u>   7) <u>II Kings</u>   8) <u>I Chronicles</u>

    9) <u>II Chronicles</u>   10) <u>Ezra</u>   11) <u>Nehemiah</u>   12) <u>Esther</u>

The next section in the Old Testament makes up <u>five</u> books and these are called the books of <u>Poetry</u>.

l) <u>Job</u>   2) <u>Psalms</u>   3) <u>Proverbs</u>   4) <u>Ecclesiastes</u>   5) <u>The Song of Solomon</u>

The next section of the Old Testament makes up <u>five</u> books also and is called the <u>Prophets Major</u>.

l) <u>Isaiah</u>   2) <u>Jeremiah</u>   3) <u>Lamentations</u>   4) <u>Ezekiel</u>   5) <u>Daniel</u>

The last section in the Old Testament makes up <u>twelve</u> books also and is called the <u>Prophets Minor</u>.

    1) <u>Hosea</u>   2) <u>Joel</u>   3) <u>Amos</u>   4) <u>Obadiah</u>

    5) <u>Jonah</u>   6) <u>Micah</u>   7) <u>Nahum</u>   8) <u>Habakkuk</u>

    9) <u>Zephaniah</u>   10) <u>Haggai</u>   11) <u>Zechariah</u>   12) <u>Malachi</u>

There are a total of <u>39</u> Old Testament books. And there are how many sections that make up the Old Testament? <u>Five</u>

How many books are in each of these sections?

Section 1	<u>Pentateuch</u>	=	<u>5</u>
Section 2	<u>Past History</u>	=	<u>12</u>
Section 3	<u>Poetry</u>	=	<u>5</u>
Section 4	<u>Prophets Major</u>	=	<u>5</u>
Section 5	<u>Prophets Minor</u>	=	<u>12</u>

By learning this, it will help us in knowing the theme of the book in which we are reading.

It will also help us be more familiar with our Bible. We now come to 400 silent years in the Word of God. Then we have the writings of the New Testament.

The New Testament is broken up into four sections. Many times we call Matthew, Mark, Luke, and John the gospels. But in section 1 we are going to add the book of Acts to make a total of five books in the first section. Remember Acts was written by the Apostle Luke and literally becomes an extension of the book of Luke.

The first section in the New Testament makes up five books and is called History.

    1) Matthew   2) Mark   3) Luke   4) John   5) Acts

The next section in the New Testament makes up fourteen books and is called the Pauline Epistles.

Why do you think they are called this? Because Paul wrote them!

    1) Romans   2) I Corinthians   3) II Corinthians   4) Galatians

    5) Ephesians   6) Philippians   7) Colossians   8) I Thessalonians

    9) II Thessalonians   10) I Timothy   11) II Timothy

    12) Titus   13) Philemon   14) Hebrews

The next section in the New Testament makes up seven books and is called the General Epistles.

    1) James   2) I Peter   3) II Peter   4) I John

    5) II John   6) III John   7) Jude

The last section in the New Testament only accounts for one book and that book in this section is called Revelation.

    1) Revelation

Revelation is also known as Apocalypse. It is the last book of the Bible which points to future events. It is written to encourage the saints in their faithful walk, and to make the sinners stop and think about their future.

There are a total of <u>27</u> New Testament books. And there are how many sections that make up the New Testament? <u>Four</u>.

Section 1	<u>History</u>	= <u>5</u>
Section 2	<u>Pauline Epistles</u>	= <u>14</u>
Section 3	<u>General Epistles</u>	= <u>7</u>
Section 4	<u>Revelation</u>	= <u>1</u>

* **<u>The Codes of the Scriptures</u>**   (Names) 24 listed in Psalms 119

(VS 1) * <u>The Law of the Lord</u>	(VS 2) * <u>His Testimonies</u>
(VS 3) * <u>His Ways</u>	(VS 4) * <u>Thy Precepts</u>
(VS 5) * <u>Thy Statutes</u>	(VS 9) * <u>Thy Word</u>
(VS 10) * <u>Thy Commandments</u>	(VS 13) * <u>The Judgments</u>
(VS 30) * <u>Way of Truth</u>	(VS 72) * <u>Law of thy Mouth</u>
(VS 88) * <u>Testimony of thy Mouth</u>	(VS 103) * <u>Honey (sweet)</u>
(VS 105) * <u>A Lamp</u>	(VS 105) * <u>A Light</u>
(VS 114) * <u>Shield</u>	(VS 127) * <u>Above Fine Gold</u>
(VS 129) * <u>Wonderful</u>	(VS 130) * <u>Understanding</u>
(VS 138) * <u>Righteous</u>	(VS 138) * <u>Very Faithful</u>
(VS 140) * <u>Pure</u>	(VS 152) * <u>Founded Forever</u>
(VS 160) * <u>Endureth Forever</u>	(VS 174) * <u>Delight</u>

(Psalms 119:127) *"Therefore I love thy commandments above gold; yea, above fine gold."*

* The Word of God is also called:

<u>The Rock</u>	<u>The Bread</u>	<u>The Water</u>	<u>The Hammer</u>
<u>The Meat</u>	<u>The Milk</u>	<u>The Seed</u>	<u>The Book</u>
<u>Jesus and other names…</u>			

* **<u>The Christ in the Scriptures</u>**

(Hebrews 10:7) *"Then said I, Lo, I come (in the volume of the book it is written of me,) to do thy will, O God."*

(John 1:1, 14) *"In the beginning was the Word, and the Word was with God, and the Word was God."*

(VS 14) *"And the Word was made flesh, and dwelt among us..."*

Jesus Christ is the volume of the book, or the filling of the book. God's love is displayed in the Old Testament as He points forward to His Son. For example:

Genesis -

> * The shedding of innocent animals to cover Adam and Eve's sin.
>
> * The honoring of Abel's blood sacrifice.
>
> * Noah's ark being lifted up above judgment (Noah's animal sacrifices)
>
> * Melchizedek King of Salem (Jerusalem; no beginning, no ending)
>
> * The Abrahamic blood covenant (Man sleeps; God seals)
>
> * The birth of Isaac (The birth of Christ)
>
> * The sacrifice of Isaac (Jehovah - Jireh = God will supply)
>
> * The life of Joseph (Saves his family, a great picture of Christ)

In Exodus 12 we see the Passover as Moses tells God's children to take <u>a lamb</u>, <u>the lamb</u>, <u>your lamb</u>, and then they are to take the <u>blood</u> and put it upon their house, the two side posts and on the upper door post, taking the lamb inside and eating it. Then the death angel, when it sees the <u>blood</u> will pass over that house. (What a picture of Christ.)

In Leviticus, we see the sin offering (The blood)

In Numbers, we see the serpent of brass (Look and live)

In Deuteronomy, we see the cities of refuge (To protect the slayer)

In Joshua we meet the unseen Captain / Rahab and the scarlet thread.

Judges represents the Godly prophet Samuel we see the anointing of David, the slaying of the giant, the blood covenant ~ Psalms 22 we see the picture of the cross in Chapter 23 we see our Shepherd.

In Solomon we see the bride and the bridegroom (Church and Christ)

In Isaiah 9 we see the great light, the Child (Jesus to be born) He is Wonderful, Councilor, the Mighty God, the Everlasting Father, the Prince of Peace... He is the volume of the Book!

In the New Testament we record His <u>Virgin Birth</u>, <u>Valiant Life</u>, <u>Vicarious Death</u>, <u>Verbal Declaration</u>, <u>Victorious Resurrection</u>, <u>Visual Ascension</u>, and His <u>Visible Return</u>. Every book talks about and points to or points ahead to His return.

- God loved us so much that He gave us His <u>Son</u>.
- Jesus loved us so much that He gave us His <u>life</u>.
- Holy Spirit loves us so much He wants to live <u>inside of us</u>.

Jesus is found <u>1028</u> times in the Word of God.

Christ is found 574 times in the Word of God.

Other names for Christ are found too numerous to even say.

He truly is the volume of the book.

<u>If you love Him you should want to read about Him!</u>

✝ We are commanded to read His word! <u>Important</u>

(II Timothy 3:16-17) *"All scripture is given by inspiration of God, and is profitable for doctrine, for reproof, for correction, for instruction in righteousness:"*

(VS 17) *"That the man of God may be perfect, thoroughly furnished unto all good works."*

(II Timothy 2:15) *"Study to shew thyself approved unto God, a workman that needeth not to be ashamed, rightly dividing the word of truth."*

Then we see the brethren at Berea:

(Acts 17:11) *"These were more noble than those in Thessalonica, in that they received the word with all readiness of mind, and searched the scriptures daily, whether those things were so."*

(Luke 4:4) Jesus said: *"...It is written, that man shall not live by bread alone, but by every word of God."*

(John 8:31) Jesus said: *"...If ye continue in my word, then are ye my disciples indeed."*

(John 14:23) Jesus said: *"...If a man love me, he will keep my words..."*

✝ (John 5:39) Jesus said *"Search the scriptures; for in them ye think ye have eternal life: and they are they which testify of me."*

We are commanded to read, study, rightly divide, keep and continue in God's Word!

Are you reading? <u>Yes</u>

We are also supposed to be changed by the Word of God.

(II Corinthians 5:17) *"Therefore if any man be in Christ, he is a new creature: old things are passed away; behold, all things are become new."*

We are to put off the old coat and put on the new!

We are to put off the old man and put on the new!

Paul said (Romans 6:7) *"For he that is dead is freed from sin."*

* We are <u>commanded</u> to read.

* We are to be <u>changed</u> from God's Word.

* We are <u>called</u> to be a witness for Him.

(Acts 1:8) *"…and ye shall be witnesses unto me…"*

C. <u>The Blessings of the Scriptures</u>

* <u>Repenting brings blessings</u>

(II Corinthians 7:10) *"For godly sorrow worketh repentance to salvation…"*

(Acts 3:19) *"Repent ye therefore, and be converted, that your sins may be blotted out, when the times of refreshing shall come from the presence of the Lord."*

(Romans 4:7-8) *"Saying, Blessed are they whose iniquities are forgiven, and whose sins are covered."*

"Blessed is the man to whom the Lord will not impute sin."

* <u>Reading brings blessings</u>

(Revelation 1:3) *"Blessed is he that readeth, and they that hear the words of this prophecy, and keep those things which are written therein: for the time is at hand.*

(Luke 11:28) *"…blessed are they that hear the word of God, and keep it."*

(James 1:25) *"But whoso looketh into the perfect law of liberty, and continueth therein, he being not a forgetful hearer, but a doer of the work, this man shall be blessed in his deed."*

* <u>Resting in Him brings blessings</u>

(Psalms 116:15) *"Precious in the sight of the Lord is the death of His saints."*

(Psalms 121:7) *"The Lord shall preserve thee from all evil: He shall preserve thy soul."*

(Revelation 14:13) *"...Blessed are the dead which die in the Lord from henceforth: Yea, saith the Spirit, that they may rest from their labours; and their works do follow them."*

* Praise God one day we will take our flight on the wings of a dove and find rest!

(Hebrews 11:21) *"By faith Jacob, when he was a dying, blessed both the sons of Joseph; and worshipped, leaning upon the top of his staff."*

* O that we could look at the staff of our life and shout and worship, the blessings of God. And then before we leave pass the blessings along! I have just barely scratched the surface on the Word of God. The Bible tells us that the worlds were framed by it, that we are saved by it. Its contents deal with issues such as: <u>Anger</u>, <u>Belief</u>, <u>Charity</u>, <u>Children</u>, <u>Comfort</u>, <u>Courage</u>, <u>Death</u>, <u>Enemies</u>, <u>Eternal Life</u>, <u>Faith</u>, <u>Fear</u>, <u>Forgiveness</u>, <u>Fruit</u>, <u>Grace</u>, <u>Guidance</u>, <u>Guilt</u>, <u>Hope</u>, <u>Hospitality</u>, <u>Illness</u>, <u>Jealousy</u>, <u>Joy</u>, <u>Kindness</u>, <u>Love</u>, <u>Lust</u>, <u>Lying</u>, <u>Marriage</u>, <u>Mercy</u>, <u>Money</u>, <u>Nature</u>, <u>Obedience</u>, <u>Peace</u>, <u>Pride</u>, <u>Prayer</u>, <u>Questions</u>, <u>Repentance</u>, <u>Salvation</u>, <u>Sex</u>, <u>Shame</u>, <u>Sickness</u>, <u>Sin</u>, <u>Success</u>, <u>Trust</u>, <u>Temptation</u>, <u>Ungodliness</u>, <u>Vices</u>, <u>Wisdom</u>, <u>Work</u>, <u>Worry</u>, <u>Worship</u>, <u>X-ray of Life</u>, <u>Yielding</u>, <u>Zealots</u> and many, many, many other <u>topics</u>, <u>situations</u> and <u>people</u>.

For extra information on what Bible to read see the following:

1) Let's Weigh The Evidence   By: Barry Burton

2) K.J.V. 1611 Perfect   By: Dr. Ray Brawson

3) Which Bible is God's Word   By: Gail Riplinger

4) Biblical Scholarship   By: Peter S. Ruckman

5) Manuscript Evidence   By: Peter S. Ruckman

6) Defending the K.J.V.   By: Dr. D.A. White

7) Final Authority   By: William P. Grady

A good study Bible may cost a little bit of money, but it's the best investment we will ever make. The following are the Pastor's picks on Study Bibles:

* 1) The Old Scofield K.J.V. Study Bible

   2) The K.J.V. Open Bible

   3) The K.J.V. Thompson Chain

   4) The K.J.V. Companion Bible

   5) The K.J.V. Reese Chronological Bible

   6) The K.J.V. Kwikscan

   7) The K.J.V. Rainbow Bible

My prayer is that you already have or get a good K.J.V. study Bible. Then secondly that you read it daily, and be a doer of the Word of God.

If you want to read along with a commentary, below are a few you might consider:

* 1) Expository Outlines on the N.T. and O.T.   By: Dr. Warren W. Wiersbe

   2) The Wycliff Bible Commentary

   3) Wilmington Guide to the Bible

   4) Matthew Henry's Commentary (1 Volume Set)

Also some other great helps for your Bible reading:

* 1) Strong's Exhausted Concordance of the Bible

   2) Young's Analytical Concordance to the Bible

* 3) Holman Bible Dictionary

   4) Vines Expository Dictionary of the O.T. and N.T.

The ones that are marked with an asterisk would be a great start to help you in your studies of the Word of God. If you are just saved, start reading in the book of John through Revelation. Then read Matthew, Mark, and Luke before you start in the Old Testament. You should at least pray and read the Bible through at least one time before using any commentaries or books that may help you. This will allow God to sink His scriptures in your heart, and place some strong preferences and convictions in your life before being influenced daily by someone else.

Books and commentaries are great, but always remember it's His Book with which one day we will be judged by.

I pray you have a burning desire to read and study His word!

ANSWERS OF THE SCRIPTURE TEST

1. What version of the Bible in English does the writer say is God's perfect Word?

   ___K.J.V.___

2. According to (Matthew 24:35) what will not pass away?

   ___God's Word___

3. There are ___39___ Old Testament Books, ___27___ New Testament Books totaling ___66___

4. How many sections is the O.T. broken into? ___5___ How many in the N.T.? ___4___

5. What chapter in Psalms gives 198 references to the word of God?

   ___Psalms 119___

6. According to (Hebrews 10:7) who is the reference to about the volume of the book?

   ___Jesus___

7. According to (Exodus 12) why do we see the death angel pass over the Israelites homes? ___Blood of the Lamb___

8. God loved us so much he gave us His ___Son___,

   Jesus loved us so much He gave us His ___Life___.

9. In the council of the scriptures we were given eight scripture references to let us know that we are commanded to do what? ___Read God's Word___

10. In (II Timothy 2:15) as a workman we are commanded to do what? ___Study___

11. We are commanded to read God's Word, but also God's Word should do what to us?

    ___Change us___

12. We talked about the three "R's" of the blessings of the scriptures, name them.

A) ___Repenting brings blessings___

B) ___Reading brings blessings___

C) ___Resting in Him brings blessings___

The Bible and the TV Guide

On the table side by side:

the Holy Bible and the TV guide.

One is well worn, but cherished with pride,

(not the Bible, but the TV guide).

One is used daily to help folks decide.

No, not the Bible; it's the TV guide.

As pages are turned, what shall they see?

Oh, what does it matter turn on the TV.

Then confusion reigns, they can't all agree

On what they shall watch on the old TV.

So, they open the book in which they confide

(no, not the Bible, it's the TV guide).

The Word of God is seldom read,

Maybe a verse e'er they fall into bed

Exhausted and sleepy and tired as can be,

Not from reading the Bible; from watching TV.

So, then back to the table, side by side,

It's the Holy Bible and the TV guide.

No time for prayer, no time for the Word.

The Plan of Salvation is seldom heard.

Forgiveness of sin so full and free,

It's found in the Bible ...not on TV.

Chapter V

SUBMERSION

(Baptism)

Baptism: (Noah Webster 1828)

l. The application of water to a person, as a sacrament or religious ceremony, by which he is initiated into the visible Church of Christ. This is usually performed by sprinkling or immersion.

2. The sufferings of Christ. Matt. XX, 22, 23

3. So much of the gospel as was preached by John the Baptist. Acts XVIII   Cruden

Baptism: (Holman's Bible Dictionary)

The immersion of dipping of a believer in water symbolizing the complete renewal and change in the believer's life and testifying to the death, burial, and resurrection of Jesus Christ as the way of salvation.

Baptism: (Vine's Expository Dictionary)

* Baptisma (noun) Baptism, consisting of the process of immersion, submersion and emergence (from bapto, to dip)...

* Baptizo (verb) To baptize, primarily a frequentative form of bapto, to dip, was used among the Greeks to signify the dying of a garment or the drawing of water by dipping a vessel into another, etc...

(I Corinthians 10:2) *"And were all baptized unto Moses in the cloud and in the sea;"*

Baptize is found <u>63</u> times in the Bible.

Baptism is found <u>26</u> times in the Bible.

Baptist is found <u>25</u> times in the Bible.

John was known as John the Baptist because he was one that baptized people at the river. He called upon people to repent, that they might receive remission of sins. Those who obeyed came "<u>confessing their sins</u>" thus acknowledging their unfitness to be in the Messiah's coming kingdom.

We see this in the four gospels and in Acts such as (Acts 1:5; 11:16; 19:4)

Distinct from this is the baptism enjoyed by Christ (Matthew 28:19) a baptism to be undergone by believers, thus witnessing to their identification with Him in death, burial and resurrection.

"Go ye therefore, and teach all nations, baptizing them in the name of the Father, and of the Son, and of the Holy Ghost:"

This would indicate that the baptized person was closely bound to, or became the property of, the one into whose name he was baptized.

A. <u>The Beginning of Baptism</u>

* <u>Noah</u> (Genesis 6) The Bible says (VS 8)

"...Noah found grace in the eyes of the Lord."

The earth was corrupt before God and He was going to baptize the earth with water, and only <u>8</u> souls would arise from this baptism.

Noah builds an ark, according to God's command. At the appointed time Noah, his wife, his three sons and their wives step inside the ark and God shuts the door of grace.

God's baptismal judgment submerges all sinners and brings death, but to Noah and his family, they are brought out alive.

* <u>Moses</u> (Exodus 2) The Bible says (VS 3)

"...she took for him an ark of bulrushes, and daubed it with slime and with pitch, and put the child therein;"

He was set in the flags of the river bank, and by God's hand of grace he was drawn out of the water, arising out of the water alive. These are the symbols of baptism.

* Moses and the Children of Israel

    1) Red Sea = (Exodus 14) Moses says in (VS 13) ***"...Fear ye not, stand still, and see the salvation of the Lord, which He will shew to you today: for the Egyptians whom ye have seen today, ye shall see them again no more forever."***

Moses then lifts up the rod of God and stretches it out over the sea, and it divides and the children of Israel go over on dry ground.

They were covered by the cloud of God, walls of water were on both sides and they were taken to the other side and brought out alive.

Then we see baptism of judgment of God as the Egyptians follow, and God closes in the water of judgment upon them as they drown in the Red Sea.

    2) Jordan River (Joshua 3) (VS 13) ***"And it shall come to pass, as soon as the soles of the feet of the priests that bear the ark of the Lord, the Lord of all the earth, shall rest in the waters of Jordan, that the waters of Jordan shall be cut off from the waters that come down from above; and they shall stand upon an heap."***

The Jordan at this time was extremely high; in fact the Bible lets us know it overflowed its banks. The people had just sanctified themselves and now as the priests' feet touch the water, the water walls up on both sides, and the cloud of God is overhead, and once again we see a beautiful picture of baptism, as the children of Israel arise alive on the other side, ready to do battle for the Lord. Then baptism flows into the New Testament, becoming a symbol to all those who repent and choose to follow Christ. This brings in the baptism of John and the baptism of Christ.

B. **The Basics of Baptism**

We are going to be looking at the basics of water baptism. Some believe that you cannot be totally saved without being baptized. Others believe you can only be baptized in the name of Jesus.

Question #1:   Is salvation by grace and baptism?

We are going to tackle these beliefs along with others from the word of God.

* The Bible says (Ephesians 2:8-9)

"For by grace are ye saved through faith; and that not of yourselves: it is the gift of God:" "Not of works, lest any man should boast."

Grace   = God's unmerited favor. (Freedom from sin through divine grace)

Faith   = our belief and trust in God; (complete trust)

Gift   = God's love given to man (John 3:16)

"For God so loved the world, that He gave His only begotten Son, that whosoever believeth in Him should not perish, but have everlasting life."

Within this verse we see the gift of God which is His Son. We see the terms of everlasting life, which is our faith believing Jesus to be the Son of God. And last we see the grace of God, doing something for us, for which we are so undeserving.

Salvation is simply God's grace of His gift and our faith in this gift.

✝ **You cannot add to the grace of God.** ✝

(Romans 10:9-13; John 3)

Some say that you must believe by faith and then be baptized and then you are saved. Baptism though ever so small is a work unto God.

- (Ephesians 2:9) *"Not of works, lest any man should boast."*

Even from the beginning there was the debate about baptism. Paul wanted to put an end to this debate. (I Corinthians 1:13-18) (VS 13) *"Is Christ divided? Was Paul crucified for you? Or were ye baptized in the name of Paul?"* (VS 14) *"I thank God that I baptized none of you, but Crispus and Gaius;"* (VS 15) *"Lest any should say that I had baptized in mine own name."* (VS 16) *"And I baptized also the household of Stephanas: besides, I know not whether I baptized any other."* (VS 17) *"For Christ sent me not to baptize, but to preach the gospel: not with wisdom of words, lest the cross of Christ should be made of none effect."* (VS 18) *"For the preaching of the cross is to them that perish foolishness; but unto us which are saved it is the power of God."*

The Corinthian church was being divided over baptism. Paul was glad that he didn't baptize a lot of the believers, for they were thinking there was some special power in this.

Paul states in (verse 17) that he was sent not to baptize, but to preach the gospel.

Q. What is the difference between baptism and the gospel?

The gospel Paul goes on to explain it is the cross of Christ. This is what he has been commanded to preach and to those who believe, Paul goes on to say they are saved and the cross becomes the power of God in their lives.

Baptism is something done in following the Lord. IT IS YERY IMPORTANT! But it cannot be added to salvation. After (Ephesians 2:8-9) comes (VS 10) and here is where baptism comes in. ***"For we are His workmanship, created in Christ Jesus unto good works, which God hath before ordained that we should walk in them."***

We should follow the Lord in water baptism, it is important in a young Christian's life. Once we are saved we are created in Christ Jesus unto good works.

If it's true faith then works will follow.

(James 2:18) ***"Yea, a man may say, Thou hast faith, and I have works: shew me thy faith without thy works, and I will shew thee my faith by my works."***

Once you are saved good works must follow. Baptism is one of the first steps of good works. Remember we cannot add to our salvation, for our righteousness is as filthy rags, but salvation should give birth to good works.

✝ Jesus sets the example of water baptism ✝

and as Christians, we should follow

His example.

Question #2: Now the question arises how should one be baptized?

    1) Some anoint with water.

    2) Some sprinkle with water.

    3) Some pour on water.

    4) Others submerge in water.

The word baptism is taken from the word baptizo: immersion, its literal meaning is to dip.

Though each of these ways represents a symbol of baptism, the correct way according to the word itself would be to submerse or to totally have oneself dipped under the water.

Question #3: What are the words that should be used in water baptism?

* (John 21) Jesus command is to *"feed my sheep"*. Commanded to teach.

* (Luke 24:45-49) Jesus' call to His disciples is to preach.

(VS 47) ***"And that repentance and remission of sins should be preached in His name among all nations, beginning at Jerusalem."***

* (Mark 16:15-20) Jesus' commission (known as the Great Commission)

(VS 15) ***"And he said unto them, Go ye into the entire world, and preach the gospel to every creature."***

(VS 16) ***"He that believeth and is baptized shall be saved; but he that believeth not shall be damned."***

- Notice He does not say that if you are not baptized you will be damned. He is not saying baptism is necessary to salvation, but that the person who is saved should be baptized. It is rejection of Christ which brings damnation. (John 3:36) ***"He that believeth on the Son hath everlasting life: and he that believeth not the Son shall not see life; but the wrath of God abideth on him."***

* (Matthew 28:18-20) Jesus' commission (known as the Great Commission)

Now this is after Jesus' death and resurrection, He now gives us the pattern of baptizing in His name.

(VS 19) ***"Go ye therefore, and teach all nations, baptizing them in the name of the Father, and of the Son, and of the Holy Ghost:"***

(VS 20) ***"Teaching them to observe all things whatsoever I have commanded you: and, lo, I am with you always, even unto the end of the world. Amen."***

Jesus is setting the pattern for baptizing in His name, and this is to be done to all nations.

- Salvation is by grace through faith, not baptism.

- Baptism is an important step after salvation.

- Baptism is to dip or submerge someone in water.

- We are baptized in the name of the Father, the Son, and the Holy Ghost.

- Baptism is an outward sign to an inward change.

(Romans 6:3-5) *"Know ye not, that so many of us as were baptized into Jesus Christ were baptized into His death?"*

(VS 4) *"Therefore we are buried with Him by baptism into death: that like as Christ was raised up from the dead by the glory of the Father, even so we also should walk in newness of life.*

(VS 5) *"For if we have been planted together in the likeness of His death, we shall be also in the likeness of His resurrection:"*

Baptism is an outward sign to both sinner and saint that we start out one way completely dry, we are submerged below the liquid grave and we come up a totally different way.

Dry = Sinner

Wet = Saint

Now that we have died out to self and sin we are commanded to walk in the likeness of our Saviour.

Question #4: What hinders someone from being baptized?

The only criteria one must fulfill today before being baptized is that you first must be saved.

(Acts 8:36) *"...the eunuch said, See, here is water; what doth hinder me to be baptized?*

(VS 37) *"And Philip said, If thou believest with all thine heart, thou mayest. And he answered and said, I believe that Jesus Christ is the Son of God."*

Then Philip goes down into the water and baptizes the eunuch.

There is not an age limit on it, there is not a race nor a gender that holds the key. You can be baptized and should be baptized if you have accepted Jesus Christ as your Saviour.

IMPORTANT

Baptism is a very important step in our faith in following our Lord.

Have you been saved? Yes

Have you been baptized? Yes

Baptism is an ordinance to be practiced by the church!

Ordinance - An ordinance is an outward and visible symbolic rite commanded in the Bible to be practiced by the church which sets forth a central truth of the Christian faith.

It is a memorial or reminder of some precious historical event of great significance. (Do not mix this with sacrament.)

Sacrament Is something presented to the senses, which has the power, by divine institution, not only signifying, but also of efficiently conveying grace.

(As defined by the Roman Catholic Council of Trent in 1551)

* Remember we don't take a sacrament to obtain grace, because we have obtained grace through our faith and we simply follow God's ordinances, in an act of love and remembrance.

A Quick Look At Three Church Ordinances

1) The Lord's Supper (Communion, The breaking of bread)

This reminds us of the O.T. Passover Lamb and the N.T. Passover Lamb (Jesus Christ).

Always remember no grace is obtained in the eating of the Lord's Supper, but it is done to stir our hearts in remembrance.

Jesus said in (I Corinthians 11:24-25) *"...this do in remembrance of me."*

2) Feet Washing (John 13) This is usually done, for those that do it, with the Lord's Supper. In most churches today this is not practiced in part due to cultural change. Jesus takes water in a basin, and a towel and washes His disciples' feet.

(John 13:14) *"If I then, your Lord and Master, have washed your feet; ye also ought to wash one another's feet."*

During that time, when an honored guest would come, the master of the house would take off his sandals and wash his feet and then offer him something to eat and drink. Today we live in a different culture therefore many don't observe this ordinance. This ordinance is one of humility, and if done by the pastor to his church board men, or his deacons it will build strong Christian fellowship bonds. (Also done by congregations)

3) Baptism (Matthew 28:19) *"Go ye therefore, and teach all nations, baptizing them in the name of the Father, and of the Son, and of the Holy Ghost:"*

Baptism is, therefore, first and foremost, identification with Jesus Christ.

Believers should be baptized, for the word belief and baptism are almost inseparably linked together in the New Testament.

Belief is always assumed to be the root of which baptism becomes the fruit.

Some Interesting Facts

* (Acts 8)   We see the Ethiopian Eunuch saved and baptized.

The Ethiopian eunuch was a son of <u>Ham</u>.

* (Acts 9)   We see Saul (Paul) saved and baptized.

Saul of Tarsus was a son of <u>Shem</u>.

* (Acts 10) We see Cornelius saved and baptized.

Cornelius was a son of <u>Japheth</u>.

* We see in (Acts 2) the day of Pentecost, we begin to see a change in the scriptures.

(Acts 2:38) Peter says: ***"...Repent, and be baptized every one of you in the name of Jesus Christ for the remission of sins, and ye shall receive the gift of the Holy Ghost."***

<u>First</u> – Repent and Believe   <u>Second</u> – Baptized   <u>Third</u> – Receive the Holy Ghost

* (Acts 8) Philip preaching at Samaria

(Acts 8:12) ***"But when they believed Philip preaching the things concerning the kingdom of God, and the name of Jesus Christ, they were baptized, both men and women."***

Now the apostles hear they are receiving the word in Samaria, and they send Peter and John to Philip.

(VS 15) ***"Who, when they were come down, prayed for them, that they might receive the Holy Ghost:"***

<u>First</u> – Repent and Believe   <u>Second</u> – Baptized   <u>Third</u> – Receive the Holy Ghost

* (Acts 19) Paul meets disciples at Ephesus. These disciples had not yet received the Holy Ghost, but were baptized unto John's baptism.

When Paul expounds the scripture to them they believe.

(Acts 19:5) ***"When they heard this, they were baptized in the name of the Lord Jesus."***

"And when Paul had laid his hands upon them, the Holy Ghost came on them..."

<u>First</u> – Repent and Believe   <u>Second</u> – Baptized   <u>Third</u> – Receive the Holy Ghost

* (Acts 10) Cornelius, his kinsman and near friends (Gentiles)

Now things begin to change. Let's take a look as Peter preaches.

(VS 43) *"...that through His name whosoever believeth in Him shall receive remission of sins."*

(VS 44) *"While Peter yet spake these words, the Holy Ghost fell on all them which heard the word."*

(VS 45) *"And they of the circumcision which believed were astonished, as many as came with Peter, because that on the Gentiles also was poured out the gift of the Holy Ghost."*

(VS 46) *"For they heard them speak with tongues, and magnify God. Then answered Peter,"* (The evidence that they have received the Holy Ghost)

(VS 47) *"Can any man forbid water, that these should not be baptized, which have received the Holy Ghost as well as we?"*

(VS 48) *"And he commanded them to be baptized in the name of the Lord. Then prayed they him to tarry certain days."*

First – Repent and Believe   Second – Receive the Holy Ghost   Third – Baptize

The Gentiles believed the word of Peter as he preached about Jesus. Salvation takes place as the Holy Ghost falls upon them. They then speak in tongues giving evidence that they are saved to the believing Jews. They did not get baptized first and they did not receive the Holy Ghost by the laying on of hands. Baptism only happened after they believed, and they were baptized in the name of the Lord. (Representing Lord God, Lord Jesus and the Lord of the Spirit, the Holy Ghost) Which we are commanded by Jesus to be baptized in the name of the Father, and the Son, and of the Holy Ghost. (Matthew 28:19)

C. **The Beliefs of Baptism**

Baptism we know means to submerge or to dip, but this process is done and carried out through the ordinance of the church for the purpose of identification.

The act of baptism identifies us with Christ, and with the bride of Christ.

When looking through the Bible it is good to remember that the basic theological meaning of baptism is identification.

Let's look at nine different kinds of baptism in the New Testament. Each may be correctly defined by this word identification.

1) The baptism of Moses and Israel (O.T)

(I Corinthians 10:2) *"And were all baptized unto Moses in the cloud and in the sea;"*

2) The baptism of Sin and Suffering

(Luke 12:50; Matthew 20:20-23; Mark 10:35-45)

"But I have a baptism to be baptized with; and how am I straitened till it be accomplished!"

3) The baptism of John the Baptist

(National baptism of repentance Mark 1:4; 11:30; Matthew 3:7; 21:25…)

"John did baptize in the wilderness, and preach the baptism of repentance for the remission of sins."

4) The baptism for the Dead

(I Corinthians 15:29) *"Else what shall they do which are baptized for the dead, if the dead rise not at all? why are they then baptized for the dead?"*

This was an unscriptural and erroneous practice, this is one of the many errors and heresies that was taking place at Corinth. We know that baptism cannot save anyone and that salvation is a personal matter and could not be obtained by proxy anyway.

Paul is showing the inconsistency of the false teachers at Corinth in denying the doctrine of the resurrection and accepting the fallacy of baptism for the dead.

5) The baptism of New Converts

(Acts 2:41; 8:12; 9:18; 10:48; 16:15,33; 18:8; 19:3-5)

These show the baptism at Pentecost where 3,000 were baptized. Then those at Samaria, Gaza, Damascus, Caesarea, Philippi, Corinth and Ephesus.

6) The baptism of Wrath

(Matthew 3:11-12; 13:30; Revelation 6:16-17)

"I indeed baptize you with water unto repentance. but He that cometh after me is mightier than I, whose shoes I am not worthy to bear: He shall baptize you with the Holy Ghost, and with fire:"

"Whose fan is in His hand, and He will throughly purge His floor, and gather His wheat into the garner; but He will burn up the chaff with unquenchable fire."

> John's Baptism = Water (repentance)
> Jesus' Baptism = The Holy Ghost (salvation) To the Saint
> Jesus' Baptism = Judgment Fire (sin) To the Sinner

7) The baptism of all Christians

(I Corinthians 12:13) *"For by one Spirit are we all baptized into one body, whether we be Jews or Gentiles, whether we be bond or free; and have been all made to drink into one Spirit."*

This is the baptism of all Christians by the Holy Spirit into the body of Christ. (Salvation)

8) The baptism of Jesus Christ

(Matthew 3:13-17; Mark 1:9-11; Luke 3:21-22; John 1:31-34)

"Then cometh Jesus from Galilee to Jordan unto John, to be baptized of him." *"But John forbad Him, saying, I have need to be baptized of thee, and comest thou to me?"* *"And Jesus answering said unto him, Suffer it to be so now: for thus it becometh us to fulfil all righteousness. Then he suffered Him."* *"And Jesus, when He was baptized, went up straightway out of the water: and, lo, the heavens were opened unto Him, and He saw the Spirit of God descending like a dove, and lighting upon Him:"* *"And lo a voice from heaven, saying, This is my beloved Son, in whom I am well pleased"*

A) Baptized with water by John (Matthew 3:15)

B) Baptized with the Holy Spirit by the Father (Matthew 3:16)

Here we see the Trinity in the baptism of Jesus. Also we see the command in (Matthew 28:19) To: *"...baptizing them in the name of the Father, and of the Son, and of the Holy Ghost:"*

9) The baptism of the Holy Ghost

(Matthew 3:11) *"I indeed baptize you with water unto repentance. But He that cometh after me is mightier than I, whose shoes I am not worthy to bear: He shall baptize you with the Holy Ghost, and with fire:"*

John is explaining his baptism of water, stating that people repent and then are baptized. Then John begins to talk about Jesus, one who has all power and authority. He tells us that Jesus will baptize us with the Holy Ghost. Remember when He left He said He would not leave us comfortless. (Remember the day of Pentecost.)

(Acts 1:5) *"For John truly baptized with water; but ye shall be baptized with the Holy Ghost not many days hence.*

Jesus is going to be leaving, but He promised all believers that He would give them a comforter, and that comforter would be the Holy Ghost. The Holy Ghost was not only to be with them, but live in them.

94

✝ IMPORTANT ✝

The Baptism of the Holy Ghost = <u>Salvation</u>

(Acts 2) We see the day of Pentecost now was fully come the disciples in the upper room in one accord and in prayer. <u>Suddenly we have:</u>

      1) <u>A sound from heaven</u> (Like a mighty rushing wind)

      2) <u>Cloven tongues</u>   (Looked like fire)

      3) <u>Sat upon each of them</u>

      4) <u>And they were filled with the Holy Ghost</u>

(VS 4) *"And they were all filled with the Holy Ghost, and began to speak with other tongues, as the Spirit gave them utterance."*

Notice all those believers received the gift of the Holy Ghost. The evidence or identification for this new phenomenon was that they spake in tongues.

* <u>**Note:**</u> The baptism of the Holy Ghost <u>IS NOT</u> speaking in tongues, it is merely an identification of the Holy Ghost indwelling in believers.

Many call this gift here the gift of tongues (unknown language). A careful look at (Acts 2) lets us know that the gift was that of another language. In fact let's pick up the reading in (VS 5-8) *"And there were dwelling at Jerusalem Jews, devout men, out of every nation under heaven." "Now when this was noised abroad, the multitude came together, and were confounded, because that every man heard them speak in his own language." "And they were all amazed and marvelled, saying one to another, Behold, are not all these which speak Galilaeans?" "And how hear we every man in our own tongue, wherein we were born?"*

The miracle that took place was not in the mouth gate of the speaker, but rather the ear gate of the hearer.

This brings us to the types of tongues that we hear of today.

      1) <u>Foreign Tongues</u>   2) <u>Unknown Tongues</u>

      3) <u>Known Tongues</u>   4) <u>Prayer Tongues</u>

The foreign tongue was given and each one that heard these Galilaeans preach, heard them in their own tongue.

This kind of tongue would be very helpful today and would eliminate preachers in foreign lands from having to use an <u>interpreter</u>.

(Mark 16:17-18) Remember they were commanded, commissioned and called to preach the gospel and then to those who believe they were to baptize them.

"And these signs shall follow them that believe; in my name shall they cast out devils; they shall speak with new tongues;" "They shall take up serpents; and if they drink any deadly thing, it shall not hurt them; they shall lay hands on the sick, and they shall recover."

"These signs have followed the preaching of the gospel, but they are not signs to continue the preaching of the gospel. They disappeared even in the early church, but they do manifest themselves on some primitive mission frontiers even today. But if someone maintains that they are injunctions for today, then one must accept them all, even the drinking of the deadly poison. Even before the end of the first century, the sign gifts were no longer the credentials of the apostles. The test was correct doctrine."

(See II John 1:10) *"It is the word of God that is the great sign in this hour."*

This is a quote from Thru the Bible with J. Vernon McGee. Let's look at the scripture (II John 1:10) *"If there come any unto you, and bring not this doctrine, receive him not into your house, neither bid him God speed:"*

The doctrine is those walking in the truth, <u>The Word of God</u>.

Love one another and walk after His commandments. John warns of deceivers, and strongly urges the believers to abide in the doctrine of Christ.

(Acts 10:44-48) We see Cornelius, his household and his friends. They get saved, the Holy Spirit falls on them and as a sign to Peter and the other believing Jews they speak in tongues.

(VS 46) *"For they heard them speak with tongues, and magnify God…"*

The speaking in tongues becomes a <u>sign</u> to Peter and the others believing Jews.

Then it appears again in (I Corinthians Chapters 12, 13, 14).

Now during this early church process the Bible is being written as the events take place. Now in (I Corinthians 12) the apostle Paul begins to talk about spiritual gifts and the diversity of gifts.

1) <u>Wisdom</u>   (VS 8)

2) <u>Knowledge</u>   (VS 8)

3) <u>Faith</u>   (VS 9)

4) <u>Healing</u>   (VS 9)

5) <u>Miracles</u>   (VS 10)

6) <u>Prophecy</u>   (VS 10)

7) <u>Discerner of Spirits</u>   (VS 10)

8) <u>Tongues</u>   (VS:10)

9) <u>Interpretation of Tongues</u> (VS 10)

The spirit gives severally as He will! These are some of the gifts given out to the early church by direct providence of the Holy Spirit.

Then we come into (I Corinthians 13). This chapter is called the love chapter. This chapter also lets us know that some of these gifts are going to be done away with. (I Corinthians 13:8-10)

"Charity never faileth: but whether there be prophecies, they shall fail; whether there be tongues, they shall cease; whether there be knowledge, it shall vanish away." "For we know in part, and we prophesy in part." "But when that which is perfect is come, then that which is in part shall be done away."

1) Charity or <u>love</u> never faileth.

2) <u>Prophesies</u> shall fail.

3) <u>Tongues</u> shall cease.

4) <u>Knowledge</u> shall vanish away.

<u>Prophesy</u> – To foretell events, to predict, to utter predictions. There were <u>prophets</u> and <u>false prophets</u>. Of course, a <u>false prophet</u> was anyone who made a wrong prediction. Saying thus saith the Lord. (They were <u>stoned</u> and put to death.)

A true prophet is a person illuminated, inspired and instructed by God to announce future events. Such as: Moses, Elijah, David, Isaiah…

Prophesies are going to fail, tongues are going to cease, knowledge shall vanish away, the question is when?

✝ (VS 10) says *"…when that which is perfect is come…"*

What is the 'that' in (VS 10)? We know it's talking about an object and not a person, by its grammatical writing. The question then is what thing or object is perfect?

The Word of God

✝ (James 1:22-25)

(VS 25) *"But whoso looketh into the perfect law of liberty, and continueth therein, he being not a forgetful hearer, but a doer of the work, this man shall be blessed in his deed."*

✝ The Perfect Law of Liberty = The Word of God

So when the period was placed after (Revelation 22:21) the Word of God was complete. We do not need new prophesies, for all prophesy is now given and recorded in God's Word. We do not need new knowledge, for this comes from God's Word.

(Proverbs 23:12) *"Apply thine heart unto instruction, and thine ears to the words of knowledge."*

We do not need the sign nor the gift of tongues to show other believers or unbelievers for God has given us His Word, and it is complete today.

In the early church before the Word of God was complete there were instructions given to the early church in Corinth about unknown tongues. There was a warning to use this early gift right or there would be great division.

    1) Speaker of Tongues   (VS 5)   (Only with an interpreter)

    2) Interpreter of Tongues   (VS 5, 12)   (Edifying the church)

3) <u>Women were to keep silent in church</u>   (VS 34)

(They were not permitted to speak in tongues)

4) <u>Sovereign choice of spirit to give tongues to whatever man He chooses.</u>

Paul said (VS 18-19) *"I thank my God, I speak with tongues more than ye all:"* *"Yet in the church I had rather speak five words with my understanding, that by my voice I might teach others also, than ten thousand words in an unknown tongue."*

✝ <u>5</u> words of understanding over <u>10,000</u> words in an unknown tongue.

The church of Corinth had some problems; one of these was some believers thinking themselves to be more complete because they had the gift of tongues.

✝ This is a problem we have still today!

Let's go back and look at Paul's statement in (VS 18-19). He said he speaks in tongues more than them all then he says yet in church, more or less, he would rather not speak in tongues. I believe Paul was talking about prayer tongues done in privacy, between an individual and God, these tongues spoke he more than them all.

(Romans 8:26) *"Likewise the Spirit also helpeth our infirmities: for we know not what we should pray for as we ought: but the Spirit itself maketh intercession for us with groanings which cannot be uttered."*

(Jude 1:20) *"...praying in the Holy Ghost,"*

Today we have the entire Word of God and tongues, along with these others recorded in (I Corinthians 13), are no longer needed. Though they are still practiced by many I believe they were to be done away with.

Oh that men, women, boys, and girls that have given their lives to Jesus would now follow His command and be baptized. To be totally submerged in water identifying yourself with the death, burial and resurrection of Jesus Christ. (What a great thing to do). Jesus set the example of water baptism, and as Christians we should follow His example.

1) Have you been saved? <u>Yes</u>

2) Have you been baptized? <u>Yes</u>

3) What doth hinder thee? <u>Nothing</u>

ADMISSION OF THE SUBMERSION TEST

1. The word baptism comes from the word Baptizo which means? _____ To dip _____

2. In (Genesis 6) who did we see become lifted up out of a world baptism? _8 souls_ _Noah and his family_

3. When we were looking at the children of Israel what two bodies of water did we see used to illustrate baptism? A. _Red Sea_ B. _Jordan River_

4. When going over the basics of baptism we learned that you're saved by what alone? _Grace_

5. Salvation is by grace and water baptism. True or <u>False</u>

6. In the basics of baptism, we listed four ways of baptism today, list them.
A. _Anoint_ B. _Sprinkle_ C. _Pour_ D. _Submerge_

7. Given in (Matthew 28:19) what words did Jesus command that we should baptize believers in today? _The Father, the Son, and the Holy Ghost_

8. In Acts chapter 10 the baptism of Cornelius and his family and friends, we see a change in baptism. Instead of: A. Repenting and believing B. Baptized C. Receiving the Holy Ghost, we now see A. _Repenting and believing_ B. _Receiving the Holy Ghost_ C. _Baptizing_

9. In part C of the beliefs of baptism and the showing of nine different kinds of baptism, list three of them. Example: <u>The Baptism of Moses and Israel</u>
A. _Baptism of John the Baptist_ B. _Baptism of sin and suffering_
C. _Baptism for the dead_ D. _Baptism of new converts_
E. _Baptism of wrath_ F. _Baptism of all Christians_
G. _Baptism of Jesus Christ_ H. _Baptism of the Holy Ghost_

10. The baptism of the Holy Ghost is? _Salvation_

11. According to (I Corinthians 13) what three things will vanish or cease when that which is perfect is come? A. _Prophesies_ B. _Tongues_ C. _Knowledge_
According to (James 1) what is that which is perfect? _The Word of God_
or _The law of liberty_

12. According to (I Corinthians 14) Paul says he would rather in church speak 5 words with understanding than 10,000 words in an unknown tongue.

* We that are saved are commanded to be baptized by water. Have you been baptized?

<u>Yes</u>

We must follow Jesus as
good Christians of the cross.
And the first step is that of
Water Baptism.

If we cannot follow our
Lord and Master in this,
It will be very likely that
we will not follow Him in other
Steps of Life.

Moreover it is required in a
Steward that a man be found
Faithful.

God help us to be faithful in following You!

Chapter VI

STEWARDSHIP

Tithing (Noah Webster 1828)

(N) The tenth part of anything; but appropriately, the tenth part of the increase annually rising from the profits of land and stock, allotted to the clergy for their support.

Tithes are personal, predial, or mixed; personal, when accruing from labor, art, trade and navigation; predial, when issuing from the earth, as hay, wood and fruit; and mixed, when accruing from beasts, which are fed from the ground.

(V) To levy a tenth part on: to tax to the amount of a tenth. When thou hast made an end of tithing all the tithes of thine increase. Deut. XXVI

Ye must tithe mint and rue. Luke XI

To pay tithe; taxed a tenth.

Tithing levying a tax on, to the amount of a tenth.

Stewardship A steward is a man employed in great families to manage the domestic concerns, superintend the other servants, collect the rents or income, keep the accounts. See Gen. XVZ-XLIII.A.

In the scriptures and theology, a minister of Christ, where duty is to dispense the provisions of the gospel, to preach its doctrines and administer it ordinances. ...I Corth.IV

Tithe is found some 34 times in the Word of God.

Offering is found some 832 times in the Word of God.

Giving is found over 1,900 times in the Word of God.

✝ (I Corinthians 4:1-2) *"Let a man so account of us, as of the ministers of Christ, and stewards of the mysteries of God." "Moreover it is required in stewards, that a man be found faithful."*

In the New Testament a steward was the manager of a household or estate. He was appointed by the owner and entrusted to keep the estate running smoothly. Both Paul and Peter write with this thought in view, reminding us we are God's stewards. Our estate responsibilities entrusted to us are threefold. Let's take a look at each of these.

A. How we use our time

(Luke 12:42) Jesus tells a parable of faithful stewards who make good use of their time and look for Jesus' return. Then Peter asked a question to Jesus saying: *"Speakest thou this parable unto us, or even to all?"* (VS 42) *"And the Lord said, Who then is that faithful and wise steward, whom his lord shall make ruler over his household, to give them their portion of meat in due season?"*

Pastor David Jeremiah writes:

"There is a gift which comes to us from a royal source each day of our lives, bright and sparkling, absolutely, untouched, unspoiled. What is this gift?

The priceless gift of time. Each day we receive a fresh, new supply ~

24 hours, 1,440 minutes, 86,400 seconds."

* Yesterday is gone, tomorrow is uncertain, today is the time God has given us to live in.

Let's use life as being a clock. The average life span today equals seventy two years of age.

That means every three years equals one hour.

So at 18 years of age it is 6:00 AM.

At 36 years of age it is 12:00 PM.

We have now reached halfway on our life's clock of time. Where do you fit in at on the average clock of life?

My Age _____

Life's Time _____

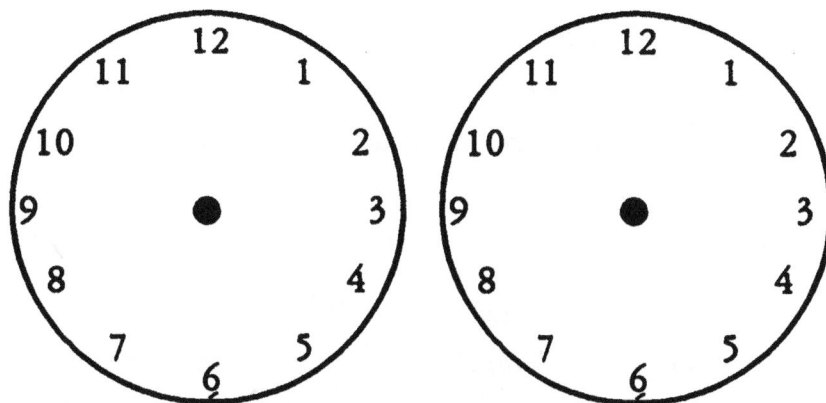

At 37 years of age you jump clocks and at <u>54</u> years of age it is <u>6:00 PM</u>.

Then at <u>72</u> years of age it is <u>Midnight</u>.

* Too soon today is tomorrow, too soon then yesterday. Let's live for God on the time of life.

We see in God's Word the importance that He places on the stewardship of time.

    1. <u>Shadow</u> (I Chronicles 29:15)

"For we are strangers before thee, and sojourners, as were all our fathers: our days on the earth are as a shadow, and there is none abiding."

    2. <u>Swift</u> (Job 7:6)

"My days are swifter than a weaver's shuttle, and are spent without hope."

    3. <u>Short</u> (Psalms 89:47-48)

"Remember how short my time is: wherefore hast thou made all men in vain?"

"What man is he that liveth, and shall not see death? Shall he deliver his soul from the hand of the grave? Selah."

    4. <u>Spent</u> (Romans 13:11-12)

"And that, knowing the time, that now it is high time to awake out of sleep: for now is our salvation nearer than when we believed."

"The night is far spent, the day is at hand: let us therefore cast off the works of darkness, and let us put on the armour of light."

5. Spray (James 4:14-15)

"Whereas ye know not what shall be on the morrow. For what is your life? It is even a vapour, that appeareth for a little time, and then vanisheth away."

"For that ye ought to say, If the Lord will, we shall live, and do this, or that."

6. Sojourning (I Peter 1:17)

"And if ye call on the Father, who without respect of persons judgeth according to every man's work, pass the time of your sojourning here in fear:"

It goes on to tell us we were not redeemed with corruptible things such as silver and gold but rather by the precious blood of Christ. Therefore in this journey of life we are not to go after the things that will cease such as our job, career, cars, houses, or money, but we should rather put Christ first and He will give us the things that we need.

Let's look at a few other scriptures that tell us what to do with this precious time.

* We should redeem the time! (Recover, ransom, rescue...)

(Ephesians 5:16) *"Redeeming the time, because the days are evil."*

(Colossians 4:5) *"Walk in wisdom toward them that are without, redeeming the time."*

- Our prayer should be that God would help us to be good stewards of this thing called time.

(Psalms 39:4-5) *"Lord, make me to know mine end, and the measure of my days, what it is: that I may know how frail I am."*

"Behold, thou hast made my days as an handbreadth; and mine age is as nothing before thee: verily every man at his best state is altogether vanity. Selah."

Time is a short passage through the gate called Eternity!

B. **How we use our talents**

(I Peter 4:10) *"As every man hath received the gift, even so minister the same one to another, as good stewards of the manifold grace of God."*

1. Precious gifts of Grace (Romans 12:6-8)

"Having then gifts differing according to the grace that is given to us, whether prophecy, let us prophesy according to the proportion of faith;" "Or ministry, let us wait on our ministering: or he that teacheth, on teaching;" "Or he that exhorteth, on exhortation: he that giveth, let him do it with simplicity; he that ruleth, with diligence; he that sheweth mercy, with cheerfulness."

Here in Romans Chapter 12 we have the gifts to the church. These gifts are to be used today. Every Christian through God's grace has received this fruit of love. Now we are to use our domineering gift to the fullest of its spiritual strength within the church.

    1) Prophecy (Preaching)

    2) Serving

    3) Teaching

    4) Exhorter

    5) Giving

    6) Organizer

    7) Mercy

Every born again Christian has some of these gifts but there should be one that is more dominating than the rest. We should find our natural gift and use it for the glory of God. Below you will find a test given by Gothard at his seminars on the gifts. Put a check in the box only if it sounds strongly like you. Then add up the totals in each section.

The answers are as follows according to the test:

Person 1 _____Teacher_____ Person 2 _____Organizer_____ Person 3 _____Prophet_____

Person 4 _____Mercy_____ Person 5 _____Exhorter_____ Person 6 _____Server_____

Person 7 _____Giver_____

Which person did you check the most? You need to read and study and use your primary gift for the glory of God.

WHICH OF THESE SEVEN PERSONS BEST DESCRIBES YOU?

Person 1

1. ☐ You want to make sure that statements are true and accurate.
2. ☐ You desire to gain as much knowledge as you can.
3. ☐ You react to people who make unfounded statements.
4. ☐ You check the credentials of one who wants to teach you.
5. ☐ You use your mind to check out an argument.
6. ☐ You enjoy spending hours doing research on a subject
7. ☐ You like to tell others as many facts as you can on a topic.
8. ☐ You pay close attention to words and phrases.
9. ☐ You tend to be silent on a matter until you check it out.
10.☐ You like to study material in a systematic sequence.

Person 2

1. ☐ You can visualize the final result of a major undertaking.
2. ☐ You enjoy coordinating the efforts of many to reach a common goal.
3. ☐ You can break down a large task into achievable goals.
4. ☐ You are able to delegate assignments to others.
5. ☐ You see people as resources that can be used to get a job done.
6. ☐ You are willing to endure reaction in order to accomplish a task.
7. ☐ You require loyalty in those who are under your supervision.
8. ☐ You remove yourself from petty details to focus on the final goal.
9. ☐ You can encourage your workers and inspire them to action.
10.☐ You move on to a new challenge once a job is finished.

Person 3

1. ☐ You see actions as either right or wrong.
2. ☐ You react strongly to people who are not what they appear to be.
3. ☐ You can usually detect when something is not what it appears to be.
4. ☐ You can quickly discern a person's character.
5. ☐ You feel a responsibility to correct those who do wrong.
6. ☐ You separate yourself from those who refuse to repent of evil.
7. ☐ You explain what is wrong with an item before you sell it.
8. ☐ You let people know how you feel about important issues.
9. ☐ You enjoy people who are completely honest with you.
10. ☐ You are quick to judge yourself when you fail.
11. ☐ You are willing to do right even if it means suffering alone for it.

Person 4

1. ☐ You can sense when people have hurt feelings.
2. ☐ You react to those who are insensitive to other's feelings.
3. ☐ You are able to discern genuine love.
4. ☐ You desire deep friendships in which there is mutual commitment.
5. ☐ You seem to attract people who tell you their problems.
6. ☐ You find it difficult to be firm or decisive with people.
7. ☐ You tend to take up offences for those whom you love.
8. ☐ You need quality time to explain how you feel.
9. ☐ You want to remove those who cause hurt to others.
10. ☐ You often wonder why God allows people to suffer.

Person 5

1. ☐ You motivate people to become what you see they could be.
2. ☐ You like to give counsel in logical steps of action.
3. ☐ You can usually discern a person's level of spiritual maturity.
4. ☐ You enjoy working out projects to help people grow spiritually.
5. ☐ You sometimes raise expectations of results prematurely.
6. ☐ You dislike teaching which does not give practical direction.
7. ☐ You like to see facial responses of those whom you counsel.
8. ☐ You often take "family time" to counsel others.
9. ☐ You enjoy giving examples from the lives of others.
10. ☐ You soon give up on those who do not follow your counsel.
11. ☐ You find it hard to follow through on a project you have started.
12. ☐ You identify with people where they are in order to counsel them.

Person 6

1. ☐ You notice the practical needs of others and enjoy meeting them.
2. ☐ You enjoy serving to free others for more important things.
3. ☐ You are willing to neglect your own work to help others.
4. ☐ You sometimes go beyond your physical strength in serving others.
5. ☐ You can remember the like and dislikes of others.
6. ☐ You can usually detect ways to serve before anyone else can.
7. ☐ You will even use your own funds to get a job done quickly.
8. ☐ You do not mind doing jobs yourself.
9. ☐ You do not want public praise, but you do need to feel appreciated.
10. ☐ You find it difficult to say "no" to those who ask for help.
11. ☐ You like to put "extra touches" on the jobs you do.

Person 7

1. ☐ You are very frugal with money for yourself and your family.
2. ☐ You enjoy investing money in the ministries of other people.
3. ☐ You have an ability to make money by wise investments.
4. ☐ You desire to keep your giving a secret.
5. ☐ You react negatively to pressure appeals for money.
6. ☐ You like to encourage others to give with your gifts.
7. ☐ You want the ministries you support to be as effective as possible.
8. ☐ You enjoy giving to needs which others tend to overlook.
9. ☐ You sometimes fear that your gift will corrupt those who get them.
10. ☐ You desire to give gifts of high quality.
11. ☐ You enjoy knowing that your gifts were specific answers to prayer.

2. Persistency in our gift (Luke 16:10)

"He that is faithful in that which is least is faithful also in much: and he that is unjust in the least is unjust also in much."

Once again He is talking about us being faithful in what God has for us to do whether it be nursery, cleaning, teaching, singing, preaching, praying, or baking.

He wants us to be faithful.

* Keep On Keeping On!

- God has given us all a certain amount of time.

- Life's time will one day pass into eternity.

- What should we do with the time: redeem it.

- We are going to give an account how we used our time and talents.

- Romans Chapter 12 lists seven gifts for today. Not only do we have the precious

and proper gift but we should be persistent in our gift.

- Not only do we need to learn how:
  - * <u>To use our time</u>
  - * <u>To use our talents</u>   but also we need to know how:
  - * <u>To use our treasures</u>   (money)

C. **<u>How we use our treasures</u>**

Have you heard the story that tithing is an Old Testament term and was done under the law, therefore in the New Testament church age we don't need to tithe?

Let me start out by saying tithing was instituted before the law, and was to be done during the law, and is to be done still today.

In (Genesis 14) we see a man called Melchizedek King of Salem (Jerusalem) Priest of the most high God. One who had no beginning of days nor ending. Abraham armed his trained servants all <u>318</u> of them and pursues the enemy that has taken Lot and his family. He smote the enemy and took the spoil; upon his return he meets the Priest of the most high God, Melchizedek.

(VS 20) *"…And he gave him tithes of all."*

This sets the stage of the first tenth and will be expanded on with the law.

* Old Testament

    1. **<u>Percentage</u>** (Leviticus 27:30; Duet 12:6; 14:22; II Chronicles 31:5-6)

"And all the tithe of the land, whether of the seed of the land, or of the fruit of the tree, is the Lord's: it is holy unto the Lord."

When giving animals, God makes it very plain it is the firstling of the flock. Abraham took the first tenth and gave it to God and refused to take any for himself. When we give, it should be our <u>first tenth</u>! Today this would equal tithing on our gross. Before anyone gets any, God gets His part, then the government, state and local, then finally you and I. We should put God first in everything!

(Proverbs 3:9)

"Honour the Lord with thy substance, and with the first fruits of all thine increase:"

2. **Personal** (freewill)

(Deuteronomy 12:6; Exodus 36:5-7; I Chronicles 29:9)

"And thither ye shall bring your burnt offerings, and your sacrifices, and your tithes, and heave offerings of your hand, and your vows, and your freewill offerings, and the firstlings of your herds and of your flocks:"

Not only were they to tithe, they were to give offerings, help feed the priests and bring their vows and commitments to God.

3. **Place** (storehouse) (Malachi 3:10)

"Bring ye all the tithes into the storehouse, that there may be meat in mine house..."

In the Old Testament, they gave the first tenth, tithe along with freewill offerings and sacrifices. They brought them to the storehouse, that there would be meat in God's house. Today a lot of good men differ over this issue called storehouse tithing. But in differing if anything the bar is to be raised, never lowered. (Matthew 5)

(VS 27) *"Ye have heard that it was said by them of old time, Thou shalt not commit adultery:"* (28) *"But I say unto you, that whosoever looketh on a woman to lust after her hath committed adultery with her already in his heart."*

Again and again in chapter 5 it says *"It has been said"* or *"You have heard"* only to hear *"But I say unto you"* and Jesus then lifts the standard in the New Testament. God warns His people in <u>Malachi</u> that they have departed from His ordinances. They ask Him where did we depart and wherein shall we return?

✝ <u>**We Are Commanded To Tithe**</u> ✝

(Malachi 3:8) *"Will a man rob God? Yet ye have robbed me. But ye say, Wherein have we robbed thee? In tithes and offerings."* (VS 9) *"Ye are cursed with a curse: for ye have robbed me, even this whole nation."*

✝ God takes tithing and giving seriously ~ Do you? <u>Yes</u>

* New Testament

In the New Testament there are <u>38</u> parables <u>12</u> of these are about money. (Over 30%)

Because 100% of what we have comes from God, we are responsible to use it all wisely and in accordance with God's will. Like every other area of stewardship, God is interested in the whole picture, not just a percentage. What we do with all our treasure is important to Him!

* Jesus dealt with money matters, because money matters!

1. <u>Prerequisite</u> of giving. The giver is first of all to have given themselves to God. God desires the dedication of our <u>wills</u> before that of our <u>wallets</u>.

This is true in both the Old and New Testament.

(Romans 12:1; II Corinthians 8:5; Psalms 26:1...)

Brethren *"...that ye present your bodies a living sacrifice, holy, acceptable unto God, which is your reasonable service."*

2. <u>Percentage</u> of giving. This is still the same. A required first <u>10%</u> tithe along with our offerings. (Matthew 23:23; Luke 11:42; 18:12...)

"Woe unto you, scribes and Pharisees, hypocrites! For ye pay tithe of mint and anise and cumin, and have omitted the weightier matters of the law, judgment, mercy, and faith: these ought ye to have done, and not to leave the other undone."

Jesus commands them on tithing even the very smallest amounts, and condemns them in other areas. Nowhere does Jesus abolish tithing, in fact, He commands it.

  * A lot of preachers feel they do not have to tithe because their income is from the tithe.

    * The best leader is one by example. The preacher should tithe the

<u>first tenth</u> like everyone else.

(Hebrews 7:9) *"And as I may so say, Levi also, who receiveth tithes, payed tithes in Abraham."*

It has been said that only a little over <u>30%</u> of the evangelical Bible believing preachers tithe their gross pay. No wonder tithing is not taught behind our pulpits today.

God is not pleased whether it be the <u>preacher</u> or the <u>people</u> who do not tithe.

3. <u>Place</u> O.T. it was the storehouse, then it was the temple and today it is the church. We are supposed to support our local church from which our souls draw their weekly strength. (Mark 12:41-42; Luke 21:1-4) *"And Jesus sat over against the treasury, and beheld how the people cast money into the treasury: and many that were rich cast in much." "And there came a certain poor widow, and she threw in two mites…"*

It wasn't much, but it was all she had!

O how Jesus loved her sacrificial gift as she brought it into the house of God.

4. <u>Pattern</u> (II Corinthians 8)

<u>The Church</u> (VS 1-3) *"…great trial of affliction the abundance of their joy and their deep poverty abounded unto the riches of their liberality…"*

They were willing even" in the hard times to make sure they gave knowing God would bless it.

<u>The Christ</u> (VS 9) *"For ye know the grace of our Lord Jesus Christ, that, though He was rich, yet for your sakes He became poor, that ye through His poverty might be rich."*

Here is the ultimate pattern for giving!

5. <u>Plan</u> (I Corinthians 16:2)

"Upon the first day of the week let every one of you lay by him in store, as God hath prospered him, that there be no gatherings when I come."

Bring your tithes and offerings in every Sunday, the first day of the week. As God has greatly blessed and prospered you, now give unto Him.

6. <u>Privileged</u> (Psalms 50:12-15) It is a privilege to give!

"If I were hungry, I would not tell thee: for the world is mine, and the fulness thereof."

"Will I eat the flesh of bulls, or drink the blood of goats?"

"Offer unto God thanksgiving; and pay thy vows unto the most High:"

"And call upon me in the day of trouble: I will deliver thee, and thou shalt glorify me."

God does not need our money! But He has graciously allowed us to give back to Him ~ and actually get credit for that which is already His.

7. Pleasure (II Corinthians 9:7)

"Every man according as he purposeth in his heart, so let him give; not grudgingly, or of necessity: for God loveth a cheerful giver."

God loves those who are happy about their tithes and offerings. With this kind of a giving heart, God will truly bless this individual.

- Do you tithe the first tenth of your income? Yes
- Do you bring your tithes in on the first day of the week? Yes
- Do you count it a privilege to tithe, and not a sacrifice? Yes
- Do you find great pleasure in giving back to God what He has blessed you with? Yes
- If you do not tithe, are you in financial trouble? N/A
- Do you believe your paycheck is truly yours or is it God's? God's
- Does God love a cheerful giver? Yes

8. Purpose The purpose of giving is at least fivefold.

* First   So that other Christians follow your pattern, so that they are challenged by how God blesses you as you give to Him.

(II Corinthians 9:2) ***"For I know the forwardness of your mind, for which I boast of you to them of Macedonia, that Achaia was ready a year ago; and your zeal hath provoked very many."***

Have a zeal and devotion in your giving, and watch how God will use you to encourage and challenge others.

* Second   So that the Father might be praised. Ultimately everything we do should be for the glory of God, so God's name will be glorified.

(II Corinthians 9:12) ***"For the administration of this service not only supplieth the want of the saints, but is abundant also by many thanksgivings unto God;"***

Many people tithe and give offerings in church and then turn around and help someone many times on their own. Then the person who receives the help thanks the kind individual Christian who helped them out. This is great and praise God for all those who help the needy in their time of trouble.

Think about this: Give your love offering to the church in care of the need that is present. When the person in need receives the help they thank the church and glorify God, not knowing the individual. But God knows.

* Third   So God's man will have a paycheck. (I Timothy 5:17-18) *"Let the elders that rule well be counted worthy of double honour, especially they who labour in the word and doctrine." "For the scripture saith, thou shalt not muzzle the ox that treadeth out the corn. And, the labourer is worthy of his reward."*

The Pastor that studies, visits, prays, and preaches the gospel is worthy of support. Even to that of double honor. Do you count it a privilege to be able to help support the man of God?

This is another one of the purposes of tithing along with upkeep and maintenance in the house of God, and other important ministries within the church.

* Fourth   So that needy saints may have provisions. (Acts 11:29)

"Then the disciples, every man according to his ability, determined to send relief unto the brethren which dwelt in Judaea:"

(I John 3:17) *"But whoso hath this world's good, and seeth his brother have need, and shutteth up his bowels of compassion from him, how dwelleth the love of God in him?"*

God's people are to help one another in prayer and in deed. A lively tithing and active church has provisions to help those in need.

* Fifth   That our lives would show prosperity.

God wants to bless us, when we cheerfully do what He has commanded us to do. We also do above that which is required, God seeks to pour His blessing out on us in abundance, for God loves those that give. (Luke 6:38) *"Give, and it shall be given unto you; good measure, pressed down, and shaken together, and running over, shall men give into your bosom. For with the same measure that ye mete withal it shall be measured to you again."*

(II Corinthians 9:6) ***"But this I say, he which soweth sparingly shall reap also sparingly; and he which soweth bountifully shall reap also bountifully."***

(Malachi 3:10) ***"Bring ye all the tithes into the storehouse, that there may be meat in mine house, and prove me now herewith, saith the Lord of hosts, if I will not open you the windows of heaven, and pour you out a blessing, that there shall not be room enough to receive it."***

(Proverbs 3:9-10) ***"Honour the Lord with thy substance, and with the firstfruits of all thine increase:" "So shall thy barns be filled with plenty, and thy presses shall burst out with new wine."***

Above there are a couple verses in both the New and Old Testament showing how God wants to give prosperity to those who give of their tithes and offerings.

* Some people say, I just can't tithe because I have too many bills or maybe that you have just been laid off from work. You say it just does not work out on paper, my need is too great, therefore I cannot give.

✝ **<u>My Testimony</u>** ✝

I cannot tell you what to do but I can give you a testimony of my early Christian life. I was saved on February 11, 1979. I then got married in the summer of 1980. My wife and I bought a house and had a new car and a new truck, everything seemed to be going great. I remember hearing a message on tithing being the first, the best, and that you should give God your first which would be your gross pay. This is before Uncle Sam or anyone else gets their portion out of it. I talked to my wife letting her know what I heard, and that it was Biblical and from that day to this God has allowed us to tithe our gross. It is always the first check written out before any others.

We still give to offerings and help support other ministries, but these are always above and beyond our tithes. It wasn't long in my Christian walk that this conviction would be tested. After about a year or so of things going great, I got laid off from work. Because of not being a good steward, I had two car payments and a house payment and little to no savings. My wife and I prayed and decided we would not stop tithing our gross to God,

118

and we asked Him to help us in our time of need. For the next year I found myself looking for a new permanent job. Many times my wife and I would gather around the coffee table wondering where we were going to come up with the payments. Time after time miraculous things would happen.

Once a lady in the church sent us a check for the exact amount for one of our bills. She stated that she knew it was an odd amount but this is what God put so heavy on her heart to send us. I was able to work some odd jobs to allow me to make exactly what I needed in finances.

Once we thought for sure we were going to be late on some bills and the pastor of our church said he felt they should take up a love offering for us. Once again God supplied our needs. Through the trial of fire I saw again and again the loving hand of God upon our lives. I count it a privilege to be able to give to God what He has so wonderfully blessed me with. God wants to show us the concept of seed and harvest. If we are willing to sow, He will allow us to reap the harvest. Praise God!

How about sitting down with your family and making a Biblical decision to give back to God your tithes and offerings? This must be done with a glad heart, for God looks at the heart of the giver. If this is done with a rejoicing heart, may I say like Moses:

"Stand Back And See The Salvation Of The Lord."

Two things in closing we should take a look at as being a good steward.

1. How do I save money?

A) Prepare (Proverbs 30:25)

"The ants are a people not strong, yet they prepare their meat in the summer;"

(Put some away in the good times for rainy days.)

B) Place (Matthew 25:27)

"Thou oughtest therefore to have put my money to the exchangers, and then at my coming I should have received mine own with usury.

(Don't stuff it under your pillow, at least let it draw interest in the bank.)

C) Plan (James 4:13-17)

Our life is a vapor, we should always plan our life in the expectation of Jesus Christ's return. (Have a balance.)

2. How do I spend money?

A) Pay (Pay your debts) (Romans 13:8; II Kings 4:7; Matthew 17:24)

(Romans 13:8) *"Owe no man anything..."*

(Matthew 17:24-25) *"...they that received tribute money came to Peter, and said, Doth not your master pay tribute?" "He saith, Yes…"*

We are to pay our debts and we are to pay our taxes.

B) Provide (Provide for your family) (I Timothy 5:8)

"But if any provide not for his own, and specially for those of his own house, he hath denied the faith, and is worse than an infidel."

We are to make sure our families have food, clothing, and a place to sleep. This is the love of Christ, this we do by faith in Him, and if we don't we have denied the faith.

C) Pleasure (Short times to get away, "vacations") (Ecclesiastes 2:24)

"There is nothing better for a man, than that he should eat and drink, and that he should make his soul enjoy good in his labour. This also I saw, that it was from the hand of God."

If at all possible try and save out enough money to go somewhere once a year for a week or weekend to rest and enjoy life which God has given.

Addressing The Stewardship Test

1. According to (I Corinthians 4:1-2) it is required in a steward that a man be found what? _____Faithful_____

2. We are to be faithful in our time spent for God because according to (James 4:14) our life is like a ____Vapor_____

3. Time is a short passage to the gate of what? _____Eternity_____

4. Part A showed us as stewards how to use our time, while part B showed us how to use our what? ____Talents_____

5. According to (Romans 12:6-8) there are seven gifts given to the church.

Example: A) Prophesy (preaching) Please list as many of the other six as you can!

B. ___Serving___ C. ___Teaching___ D. ___Exhorting___

E. ___Giving___ F. ___Organization___ G. ___Mercy___

6. Part A showed us as stewards how to use our <u>time</u> and part B showed us how to use our <u>talents</u>, part C showed us how to use our what? ___Treasures___

7. In (Malachi 3:8) what were the people guilty of robbing God in? ___Tithes___ and ___Offerings___

8. In the New Testament the storehouse becomes what? ___The Church___

9. In the New Testament over what percentage of the parables talk about money? __30%__

** <u>Jesus dealt with money matters, because money matters!</u>

** <u>Money is not the root of all evil but rather the love of money!</u>

10. Tithing the first tenth along with offerings is required. True or False

11. God wants to give prosperity to those who give of tithes and offerings. True or False

12. In the last section we went over 1. <u>How to save money</u>

A) Prepare   B) Place   C) Plan

And part 2. <u>How do I spend money</u>

A. ___Paying___ B. ___Provide___ C. ___Pleasure___

One has to do with taxes and bills and the next two with our family.

Heaven's Grocery Store

I was walking down life's highway a long time ago,

One day I saw a sign that read Heaven's Grocery Store,

As I go a little closer, the door came open wide,

And when I came to myself I was standing inside.

I saw a host of angels, they were standing everywhere,

One handed me a basket and said, "My child shop with care."

Everything a Christian needed was in that Grocery Store,

And all you couldn't carry, you could come back the next day for more.

First I got some Patience, Love was in the same row,

Further down was Understanding, you need that everywhere you go,

I got a box or two of Wisdom, a bag or two of Faith,

I just couldn't miss the Holy Ghost for He was all over the place.

I stopped to get some Strength and Courage

To help me run this race,

By then my basket was getting full,

But I remember I needed some Grace.

I didn't forget Salvation, for Salvation, that was free,

So, I tried to get enough of that to save both you and me,

Then I started up to the counter to pay my grocery bill,

For I thought I had everything to do my Master's will.

As I went up the aisle I saw Prayer and I just had to put that in,

For I knew when I stepped outside, I would run right into sin,

Peace and Joy were plentiful, they were on the last shelf,

Song and Praises were hanging near so I just helped myself.

Then I said to the Angel, "Now how much do I owe?"

He just smiled and said, "Just take them everywhere you go."

Again, I smiled at him and said, "how much, now do I really owe?"

He smiled again and said,

"My child, Jesus paid your bill a long time ago."

Chapter VII

SANCTIFICATION

Sanctification: (Noah Webster 1828)

1. The act of making holy, in an Evangelical sense, the act of God's grace by which the affections of men are purified or alienated from sin and the world, and exalted to a supreme love to God.

God hath from the beginning chosen you to salvation, through sanctification of the Spirit and belief of the truth. 2 Thess ii I Pet i

2. The act of consecrating or setting apart for sacred purpose.

Sanctified: made holy; consecrated; set apart for sacred services / affectedly holy.

Sanctify:

1. In a general sense, to cleanse, purify or make holy.

2. To separate, set apart appoint to a holy, sacred or religious use.

God blesseth the seventh day and sanctified it Gen ii

3. To purify;... 4. To separate;... 5. To cleanse from corruption;...

6. To make means of holiness;... 7. To make free from guilt;... 8. To secure from violation;...

Sanctifying: Making holy; (The process)

Sanctification is found 126 times in the Word of God.

Holiness is found 44 times in the Word of God.

Here are a few other words that are associated with Sanctification.

1. Separation
2. Consecration
3. Dedication
4. Sacred
5. Holy
6. Clean
7. Perfection

Let's first find out how one is sanctified!

We will see once again the trinity of God as we look at this!

* **God** The Father (Jude 1)

"...to them that are sanctified by God the Father, and preserved in Jesus Christ, and called..."

* **Jesus** The Son (I Corinthians 1:2)

"Unto the church of God which is at Corinth, to them that are sanctified in Christ Jesus, called to be saints, with all that in every place call upon the name of Jesus Christ..."

* **Holy Ghost** (Romans 15:16)

"That I should be the minister of Jesus Christ to the Gentiles, ministering the gospel of God, that the offering up of the Gentiles might be acceptable, being sanctified by the Holy Ghost."

* We see the sanctification of God the Father, Jesus Christ the Son, and the Holy Ghost (3 in 1)

* Today this is all done through the grace of God through His Holy Word.

<u>**Truth**</u> (God's Word) (John 17:17-19; I Timothy 4:5)

Jesus said *"Sanctify them through thy truth: thy word is truth."*

"As thou hast sent me into the world, even so have I also sent them into the world."

"And for their sakes I sanctify myself, that they also might be sanctified through the truth."

A. <u>**Positional Sanctification**</u>

* God's <u>Word</u> brings us salvation and sanctification

* God's <u>Grace</u> brings us salvation and sanctification.

* God's <u>Blood</u> brings us salvation and sanctification.

Praise God, the Word of God teaches us that we are saved by grace through faith and the blood that Jesus shed at Calvary was not only His blood but that of His Father's. (Acts 20:28)

"Take heed therefore unto yourselves, and to all the flock, over the which the Holy Ghost hath made you overseers, to feed the church of God, which He hath purchased with His own blood."

Whose church is it? = <u>**God's**</u>

<u>"Which He"</u> (who)? = <u>**God**</u>

<u>"Hath purchased with His"</u> (who's)? = <u>**God's**</u>

<u>"Own blood"</u> The Father's blood flowing through the veins of His Son. This is why Jesus was the perfect sacrifice, the Lamb of God. When Jesus said <u>*"It is finished"*</u>, He was referring to the <u>Plan of Salvation</u>. No longer would the <u>Old Testament</u> sacrifice of <u>covering</u> be needed.

Now we have the <u>New Testament</u> sacrifice which <u>cleanses</u>.

(Hebrews 10:29) *"Of how much sorer punishment, suppose ye, shall he be thought worthy, who hath trodden under foot the Son of God, and hath counted the blood of the covenant, wherewith he was sanctified, an unholy thing, and hath done despite unto the Spirit of grace?"*

* Have you been saved? Born again? And bought by the blood of Jesus? <u>Yes</u>

If you have said <u>yes</u> then <u>salvation</u> has brought a change in your life. Old things have passed away and behold all things have become new.

* There is a separation from the old life, and a <u>clean</u> and new life has begun.

* <u>Sanctification</u> has now become part of your life in Christ. Salvation has placed you in the position of sanctification in Christ. It is all part of the beautiful grace of God which He has given to us.

Some believe that this is not only where sanctification begins, but that this is where it also ends. They only believe in the position of sanctification through salvation only!

To me it is not so important what your belief and doctrine is on sanctification, but rather that we live a sanctified and holy life.

If salvation puts us in <u>positional</u> sanctification then the continuance of life puts us into <u>processional</u> sanctification.

B. **Processional Sanctification**

I believe we are born into salvation and sanctification. And as in any birth, you begin as a baby.

    A) <u>Baby</u>

    B) <u>Toddler</u> to <u>Teenager</u>

    C) <u>Adult</u>

(I Peter 2:2) *"As newborn babes, desire the sincere milk of the word, that ye may grow thereby:"*

As a born again Christian, saved and sanctified, we are to desire or have a want to read God's word. As a baby wants milk, you and I should yearn for and cry for God's word. As a baby eats and grows, you and I should also eat and grow.

(II Peter 3:18) *"But grow in grace, and in the knowledge of our Lord and Saviour Jesus Christ. To Him be glory both now and forever. Amen."*

* We are to grow in this <u>salvation and sanctification</u>, grace and in knowledge of the Word of God. This grace seems to broaden, and our faith seems to increase as we grow.

Faith we know comes from hearing and hearing by the word of God.

Our faith is to continue to grow from the Word of God. In the Bible, I see at least five faiths talked about.

      1) <u>No Faith</u>   2) <u>Faith</u>   3) <u>Little Faith</u>

          4) <u>Great Faith</u>   5) <u>Perfect Faith</u>

(II Thessalonians 1:3) *"We are bound to thank God always for you, brethren, as it is meet, because that your faith groweth exceedingly, and the charity of every one of you all toward each other aboundeth;"*

Paul while growing realized there were things in his life he had to get rid of, things he used to do, he would not do any longer and the things he didn't do, he would begin doing.

Paul started dying out to <u>self</u> and living unto the <u>Saviour</u>.

(I Corinthians 15:31) *"I protest by your rejoicing which I have in Christ Jesus our Lord, I die daily."*

Paul, day after day, would die out to self and live for Jesus. This is the heart and core of <u>processional sanctification</u>.

We have looked at the <u>position</u> and the <u>process</u> of sanctification and many believe this is the complete picture of sanctification.

Once again the importance of this is not the structure or line of sanctification but rather the <u>life</u> of sanctification. (We must live it.)

At one time we were <u>fornicators</u>, <u>idolaters</u>, <u>adulterers</u>, <u>effeminate</u>, <u>abusers of oneself</u>, <u>thieves</u>, <u>covetous</u>, <u>drunkards</u>, <u>revilers</u>, <u>extortioners</u>, and just plain <u>sinners</u>.

(I Corinthians 6:11) *"And such were some of you: but ye are washed, but ye are sanctified, but ye are justified in the name of the Lord Jesus, and by the Spirit of our God."*

✝ Sinner (Noah Webster 1828)

1. One that has voluntarily violated the divine law; a moral agent who has voluntarily disobeyed any divine precept, or neglected any known duty.

2. It is used in contradistinction to saint, to denote an unregenerate person; one who has not received the pardon of his sins.

3. An offender; a criminal.

To act as a sinner; in ludicrous language.

We could say the opposite of a sinner is a saint.

A sinner is one who remains in sin.

I know this goes against many people's belief that saved people are just sinners that are saved.

   * First ~ This goes against the very definition itself.

"One who has not received the pardon of sin."

   * Second ~ Nowhere in the word of God, once you are saved, does it call you a sinner.

(I Corinthians 6:11) *"And such were some of you..."* (Past tense)

We are called: ambassadors, Abraham's seed, brethren, believers, Christians, children, fighters, pilgrims, runners, saints, soldiers... and the list goes on and on, but we are not called sinners once we've been saved.

   * Third ~ We deny the power of God's grace if we think we remain sinners once saved.

(Romans 5:20) *"Moreover the law entered, that the offence might abound. But where sin abounded, grace did much more abound:"*

✝ (Romans 6:1-2) *"What shall we say then? Shall we continue in sin, that grace may abound?"*

"God forbid. How shall we, that are dead to sin, live any longer therein?"

128

Q. Once a sinner is saved and born again do you then continue sinning? <u>No</u>
<u>"God forbid"</u> or <u>No</u>. For if we are dead to sin how or why should we live in it?

✝ I believe many Christians, born again saints, are living beneath the ✝
privilege God has set for us in His grace!

Remember we are saved and sanctified to be set apart, different from this world. If we believe we are saved to continue sinning against God ~ something is wrong!

Q. Do you believe then once you are saved that you can never sin? <u>No</u>
But you are not to practice or live in sin. You still have the freewill to sin, but remember now you have the grace not to. And if any man does sin once they are saved, Praise God, we have an advocate.
(I John 2:1-2) *"My little children, these things write I unto you, that ye sin not. And if any man sin, we have an advocate with the Father, Jesus Christ the righteous:"*
"And He is the propitiation for our sins: and not for ours only, but also for the sins of the whole world."

If we are going to be His disciples, followers, and saints, we are to keep His commandments, and obey His words. In following Jesus we are walking in His light, and not sinning.
Let's apply our hearts and minds to the will of God, and live in the grace that He has given for us. I once heard this phrase and thought it would be worth repeating.

The Bible will keep you from sin / or sin will keep you from the Bible.

Did not David say in (Psalms 119:11)
"Thy word have I hid in mine heart, that I might not sin against thee."

Remember the song?: <u>I'm just a sinner, saved by grace.</u>
Shouldn't it be?: <u>I was a sinner, now I'm saved by grace.</u>

Once saved a sinner = Past not present ~ Becomes today a saint.

* As we live a positive life in the position of salvation and sanctification, we then follow a dying out process that will lead us from a babe to a teenager to an adult in our spiritual lives.

There is a semi time form I see in the Word of God.

Remember He has called us from the milk to meat so we might show ourselves a student of the Word.

* (II Timothy 2:15) *"Study to shew thyself approved unto God, a workman that needeth not to be ashamed, rightly dividing the word of truth."*

* (Hebrews 5:12-14) *"For when for the time ye ought to be teachers, ye have need that one teach you again which be the first principles of the oracles of God; and are become such as have need of milk, and not of strong meat."*

"For every one that useth milk is unskilful in the word of righteousness: for he is a babe."

"But strong meat belongeth to them that are of full age, even those who by reason of use have their senses exercised to discern both good and evil."

* (I Corinthians 3:1-3) *"And I, brethren, could not speak unto you as unto spiritual, but as unto carnal, even as unto babes in Christ."*

"I have fed you with milk, and not with meat: for hitherto ye were not able to bear it, neither yet now are ye able."

"For ye are yet carnal: for whereas there is among you envying, and strife, and divisions, are ye not carnal, and walk as men?"

In both places, he is crying out for them to get into the Word of God. They started out as babes, and should be now be full adults eating the meat of the Word. Not only are they not adults, they are not teenagers, they are still on the milk, and young babes. (Isaiah 28:9) Among the Jews a mother would nurse their children for 3 years. (See Matthew Henry Commentary.)

* This time frame along with Jesus teaching His disciples was around 3 years.

God wants us within around three years to be of full age.

C. **Personal Sanctification**

I believe when a person has come to reach full age in his or her Christian life, that a decision needs to be made.

That person who once has accepted Jesus Christ as their <u>Saviour</u> and became babes in Christ, now accept Jesus Christ as their <u>Lord</u> and <u>Master</u>, allowing Him to now totally lead their lives. If there is going to be any real peace and security it will come from a total commitment in Christ. The <u>processional</u> sanctification will continue, but now this individual sets their sight with blinders on toward heaven.

The Old Testament word that aligns itself with sanctification is <u>consecration</u>; the definition literally meaning a death blow. I believe sanctification is the New Testament death blow, that one comes to when accepting Jesus Christ as their Lord and Master.

✝ A Total Sellout ~ A Death Blow ✝

(John 12:23-24)

Remember how certain Greeks who came up to worship at the feast desired to see Jesus. *"And Jesus answered them, saying, The hour is come, that the Son of man should be glorified."*

"Verily, verily, I say unto you, Except a corn of wheat fall into the ground and die, it abideth alone: but if it die, it bringeth forth much fruit."

The old timers, the holiness crowd, called this personal sanctification <u>a second work of grace</u>. I don't see this so much as being a second work of grace, but rather I see it as being the total work of grace.

* (Romans 12:1-2) *"I beseech you therefore, brethren, by the mercies of God, that ye present your bodies a living sacrifice, holy, acceptable unto God, which is your reasonable service." "And be not conformed to this world: but be ye transformed by the renewing of your mind, that ye may prove what is that good, and acceptable, and perfect, will of God."*

God's ultimate will is to have all of you and me. How He desires us to give Him our all. Have you made Him Lord of your life? <u>Yes</u>

131

- What was the first sanctification we talked about? <u>position</u>

- What was the second sanctification we talked about? <u>process</u>

- What was the third sanctification we talked about? <u>personal</u>

- Approximately how many years should it take to mature in Christ? <u>3 years</u>

- The Old Testament word for sanctification is? <u>consecration</u>

- The word for consecration means? <u>death blow</u>

- We should make our lives a living what? <u>sacrifice</u>

* Remember the blind man healed outside of Bethsaida (Mark 8:23-25)

"And He took the blind man by the hand, and led him out of the town; and when He had spit on his eyes, and put His hands upon him, He asked him if he saw ought."
"And he looked up, and said, I see men as trees, walking."
"After that He put His hands again upon his eyes, and made him look up: and he was restored, and saw every man clearly."

The touch of Jesus, we relate many times to that of salvation. Then why would there be a second touch? <u>So this man could see every man clearly.</u>
Through <u>salvation</u> we thank God for what He has done for us.
Through <u>sanctification</u> we ask God what we can do for others.

We begin to see the importance of a holy life, one totally committed to Jesus, one that sees souls entering eternity and not just people. One that can see faces in the flames, and not people at the mall. A heart full of love and compassion ~ The heart of Christ.
We quote (John 15:13)
"Greater love hath no man than this, that a man lay down his life for his friends."
We always say this is Jesus, who laid His life down for us. But actually this is Jesus talking of His disciples laying down the law of love and a sanctified life.

* (Revelation 3:20)
"Behold, I stand at the door, and knock: if any man hear my voice, and open the door, I will come in to him, and will sup with him, and he with Me."

Jesus is talking, saying He stands at your heart's door and knocks. If we hear His voice, and open the door to Him in our lives, He will come in and sup with us.

"I will come in to him" <u>Salvation</u>

"and will sup with him" Jesus becomes our <u>Guest</u>.

"and he with Me" Now we turn everything over to Jesus and He becomes owner and we become <u>guest</u> in our own home. This is <u>sanctification</u>.

Remember (Hebrews 10:14)

"For by one offering He hath perfected forever them that are sanctified."

<u>God</u> Thank You for the gift of grace.

<u>Jesus</u> Thank You for the cross, Thank You for the blood, Thank You for your resurrection.

Thank You for your sanctification.

✝ (II Timothy 2:21) ✝

The foundation of God standeth sure. Everyone who nameth the name of Christ is to depart from iniquity. These are vessels of honor and some of dishonor.

"If a man therefore purge himself from these, he shall be a vessel unto honour, sanctified, and meet for the Master's use, and prepared unto every good work."

This verse will take us into our next chapter of service. Have you asked God to sanctify your life, and if not, will you? <u>Yes</u>

If we are going to produce good works we should be both saved and sanctified, living for Jesus Christ.

- **Remember it's not so important what your structure and belief on sanctification is, but rather that you live a sanctified and holy life.**

Adhering to the Sanctification Test

1. The Old Testament word for sanctification is? __Consecration__

2. We are sanctified through the following:

A) ___God___   B) ___Jesus___   C) ___Holy Ghost___   D) ___The Word___

See scriptures: (Jude 1; I Corinthians 1:2; Romans 15:16; John 17:17-19)

3. The first sanctification that takes place with salvation is? ___Positional___

4. According to (Acts 20:28) who's blood purchased us? ___God's___

5. Paul talks about dying daily. We call this what kind of sanctification? __Processional__

6. According to (I Peter 2:2) desiring milk, what spiritual state are we in? __Baby__

7. List as many of the five kinds of faith as you can: A) ___No faith___   B) ___Faith___

C) ___Little faith___   D) ___Great faith___   E) ___Perfect faith___

8. Noah Webster 1828 states that a sinner is one who has not received the pardon of his sins, so therefore once we are saved, are we sinners? ___No___

See scriptures: (Romans 5:20; Romans 6:1-2; I John 2:1-2)

9. In (Psalms 119:11) what did David hide in his heart so he would not sin against God? ___Thy Word___

10. To go from a babe to a teenager to an adult spiritually it should take around how many years? ___Three___

11. The third kind of sanctification we called: ___Personal___

12. God's ultimate will for our lives is that we make our lives a living what according to (Romans 12:1-2)? ___Sacrifice___

(Joshua 3:5)

"And Joshua said unto the people,
Sanctify yourselves: for tomorrow
the Lord will do wonders among you."

Chapter VIII

SERVICE

Service: (Noah Webster 1828)

1. In a general sense, labor of body or of body and mind, performed at the command of a superior, or in pursuance of duty, or for the benefit of another. Service is voluntary or involuntary. Voluntary service is that of a hired servant or of contract, or of persons who spontaneously perform something for another's benefit. Involuntary service is that of slaves, who work by compulsion.

...5. Anything done by the way of duty, to a superior.

...9. That which God requires of man; worship; obedience, God requires no man's service upon hard and unreasonable terms.

...13. A military achievement... 15. Favor... 17. Public worship, or office of devotion, divine service was interpreted. ...19. The offices and duties of a minister of the gospel, as in church, at a funeral, marriage, &c.

Servant: One who yields obedience to another. The saints are called the servants of God, or of righteousness; and the wicked are called the servants of sin. Rom VI

* A person who voluntarily serves another or acts as his minister; as Joshua was the servant of Moses, and the apostles the servants of Christ...

Moses is called the servant of the Lord. Deut. xxxiv

True service starts in your heart, then things begin to change in your mind. To be a true servant you have to have a change in your attitude and the way you look at things.

Always remember God is more interested in our heart's motive for doing something than in what we do. Our attitude counts for more than our accomplishments.

Also, God is the only one who has a right to judge the heart. We can be a fruit inspector and see the achievements, accomplishments and works of Christians and gauge their love for Christ by what they may or may not do. But only God has a right to look at the heart and motive of every servant.

Always remember that we are not to judge others, and have no right to guess at their motives. (Matthew 7:1-2) ***"Judge not, that ye be not judged." "For with what judgment ye judge, ye shall be judged: and with what measure ye mete, it shall be measured to you again."***

God can see past all the smoke and the clouds and sees the true motive of everything that we do.

Remember <u>King Amaziah</u> (II Chronicles 25:2)

"And he did that which was right in the sight of the Lord, but not with a perfect heart."

Jesus could always read the Scribes and Pharisees and He knew the intent of their heart. But also He could read the hearts of His disciples. He knew the thoughts and motives of their hearts.

At one place the disciples begin to reason among themselves which of them should be the greatest.

(Luke 9:47) ***"And Jesus, perceiving the thought of their heart,..."*** (Jesus knows!)

The Bible says we are to have charity out of a pure heart; we are to love others with a pure heart and one day the pure in heart shall see God.

I cannot express enough where the motives for what we do for God should come from.

(Ephesians 6:6) ***"...the servants of Christ, doing the will of God from the heart;"***

✝ Do you love God? <u>Yes</u>

✝ Are you glad you are saved? <u>Yes</u>

• What motivates you to work for God? <u>It should be because of His work for you and Me. (I John 4:19)</u>

Let's draw near to God with a true heart in full assurance, everything we do should be motivated by what He did.

In the book *The Purpose Driven Life* in Chapter 34 it says that real servants serve God with a mindset of five attitudes. We are going to take just a moment and look at these five attitudes.

I) <u>Servants think more about others than about themselves</u>.

This is true humility, to focus more on other people than on oneself. When we stop focusing on our needs, we become aware of the needs around us.

(Philippians 2:4) ***"Look not every man on his own things, but every man also on the things of others."***

True joy in life seems to work like this:

J = <u>Jesus</u>

O = <u>Others</u>

Y = <u>Yourself</u>

If we can keep this pattern in our life, we can have joy as a servant of Christ. Jesus is our great example of a true servant.

(Philippians 2:7) ***"But made Himself of no reputation, and took upon Him the form of a servant, and was made in the likeness of men:"***

Remember when Jesus knelt down and washed His disciples' feet, showing the true heart of a servant, listen to His words:

(John 13:14) ***"If I then, your Lord and Master, have washed your feet; ye also ought to wash one another's feet."***

We are to be servants, serving one another with the heart of Christ. Remember in the garden once again Jesus shows us His heart of a servant as He struggled asking God if the cup could pass, but He finishes with saying never the less not my will but thy will be done.

Jesus emptied Himself by taking the form of a servant and dying for you and me.

You can't be a servant if you are full of self. There is a constant battle in service, the line is drawn: <u>Self</u> Service or <u>Savior</u> Service.

Many times we serve to get others to like us, to be admired or to achieve our own goals. Some try to use service as a bargaining tool with God;

"I'll do this for you, God, if you'll do something for me."

Real servants don't try to use God for their purpose; instead they let God use them for His purpose. Thinking like a servant is difficult because it goes against the most basic of nature called <u>selfishness</u> (I think most about me). This is why <u>humility</u> is a daily struggle and a lesson that we must learn again and again.

Q. When was the last time you emptied yourself for someone else's benefit?

II) <u>Servants think like stewards, not owners.</u>

In the Bible, a steward was a servant entrusted to manage an estate. Joseph was this kind of servant as a prisoner in Egypt.

Joseph went from the: 1) <u>Pit</u>

                                        2) <u>Potiphar</u>

(Genesis 37-50)   3) <u>Prison</u>

                                        4) <u>Palace</u>

At Potiphar's house, the Master entrusted Joseph with everything. It seemed through his faithfulness of fleeing from Potiphar's wife that he was rewarded unjustly with prison. But in his heart he knew he had done that which was right, then the jailor entrusts Joseph with his jail and we know eventually Pharaoh entrusted the entire nation to him.

Joseph kept a good servant's heart and was not destined for prison, but for the palace.

To become a real servant you are going to have to settle the issue of money. Many people are sidetracked by serving that of materialism. Money has the greatest potential to replace God in your life.

(Luke 16:13) *"No servant can serve two masters: for either he will hate the one, and love the other; or else he will hold to the one, and despise the other. Ye cannot serve God and mammon."* (God or Money) (I Timothy 6:10) *"For the love of money is the root of all evil: which while some coveted after, they have erred from the faith, and pierced themselves through with many sorrows."*

Our view on money determines our status as a servant. If we view it as God's money and Jesus as our Master then money serves us, but if we view it as our money then it becomes our master and we become its slave.

Wealth is certainly not a sin, but failing to use it for God's glory is. True servants of God are always more concerned about <u>ministry</u> than <u>money</u>.

Be a kingdom builder; invest your money to fund God's church and its mission to the world.

III) <u>Servants think about their work, not what others are doing.</u>

They don't <u>compare</u>, <u>criticize</u>, or <u>compete</u> with other servants or ministries. They are too busy with their eyes focused on the work that God has given them to do.

Remember we are all on the same team; and our goal is to bring praise and glory to God and not to ourselves. We are all different and therefore we are all given different assignments from God.

(Galatians 5:26) ***"Let us not be desirous of vain glory, provoking one another, envying one another."***

When you are truly busy serving, you don't have time to be critical of others. There is no place for petty jealousy between God's servants.

If you serve like Jesus, you can expect to be criticized. The world and even much of the church does not understand what God values.

Remember Mary who took the most valuable thing she owned and used it in service unto Jesus. (Matthew 26:10) Mary brings an alabaster box with 12 ounces of precious ointment worth some 300 pence (1 pence equaling a day's labor). This ointment was considered a year's salary. The disciples wanted it to be sold and put into the treasury. Jesus says:

(VS 10) ***"…Why trouble ye the woman? for she hath wrought a good work upon me."***
Now this has become a memorial unto her.

Your service for Christ is never wasted for God sees your heart, regardless of what others say.

IV) <u>Servants base their identity in Christ.</u>

Because they remember they are loved and accepted by grace, servants don't have to prove their worth. They willingly accept jobs that insecure people would consider "beneath" them. Remember Jesus as He washed the feet of His disciples, what an example!

If you're going to be a servant, you must settle your identity in Christ.

* Insecure people never seem to settle their salvation.

* Insecure people are always worrying how they appear to others.

* Insecure people want others to serve them.

When you base your worth and identity on your relationship to Christ, you are freed from the expectation of others.

The question in life should not be:

      * What do people think? But rather

      * What does God think? A true servant's thoughts

(II Corinthians 10:18) *"For not he that commendeth himself is approved, but whom the Lord commendeth."*

If anyone had a chance of a lifetime to make their name known by flaunting his connections it would be James the half-brother of Jesus. Yet, in introducing his letter he simply referred to himself as a servant.

(James 1:1) *"James, a servant of God and of the Lord Jesus Christ,..."*

The closer you get to Jesus, the less you need to promote yourself.

Remember when you base your worth and identity on your relationship with Christ, you are freed from the expectations of others.

V) Servants think of ministry as an opportunity not obligation.

They enjoy helping people, meeting needs, and doing ministry. They are grateful for His grace and mercy and they know serving is the highest use of life.

(Psalms 100:2) *"Serve the Lord with gladness..."*

As we serve the Lord with gladness we have a promise from God for a reward.

(John 12:26) *"If any man serve me, let him follow me; and where I am, there shall also my servant be: if any man serve me, him will my Father honour."*

(Hebrews 6:10) *"For God is not unrighteous to forget your work and labour of love, which ye have shewed toward his name, in that ye have ministered to the saints, and do minister."*

Let's take a look at a few of the rewards that await God's faithful servants.

CROWNS

1) The Incorruptible Crown (I Corinthians 9:25-27)

This is given to those who master the old nature.

2) The Crown of Rejoicing (I Thessalonians 2:19-20; Proverbs 11:30; Daniel 12:3)

This is given to all the soul winners.

3) The Crown of Life (Revelation 2:10; James 1:2-3)

This is given to those who successfully endure temptation.

4) The Crown of Righteousness (II Timothy 4:8)

This is given to those who look for and love the doctrine of the Rapture.

5) The Crown of Glory (I Peter 5:2-4; II Timothy 4:1-2; Acts 20:26-28)

This is given to faithful preachers and teachers.

We are able to win and receive these along with many other great works. (II Corinthians 5:10) *"For we must all appear before the judgment seat of Christ; that every one may receive the things done in his body, according to that he hath done, whether it be good or bad."*

* Also see (I Corinthians 3:11-15)

We are to receive all these rewards, so one day we can lay them at the feet of Jesus.

The carnal Christian will receive nothing to replace his burned up wood, hay, and stubble. Be careful because satan and self are always trying to take and steal what we have done for God. Trying to turn our good works into stubble.

(Colossians 2:18) *"Let no man beguile you of your reward..."*

(II John 1:8) *"Look to yourselves, that we lose not those things which we have wrought, but that we receive a full reward."*

(Revelation 3:11) *"Behold, I come quickly: hold that fast which thou hast, that no man take thy crown."*

Imagine what could happen if all Christians in the world got serious about their role as a real servant. Imagine all the good that would be done if every Christian would decide to become a sold out servant of the living Saviour Jesus Christ.

* The only real happy people in life are those who have learned how to serve.

I believe if we keep the mindset of these five attitudes while serving God, we will be very productive servants.

Let's look at three areas of service:

A) WORK (Servant)

While working and serving, God is looking for our faithfulness.

The Bible says that a servant is to be obedient to his master. In (Matthew 8) we see the centurion who comes to Jesus and wants his servant healed., He tells Jesus he is a man of authority, he tells his soldiers and servants to do something and they do it.

Q. Are we faithful servants? Yes

Q. Are we busy serving God? Yes

In (Matthew 25:14-30) Jesus talks about three servants.

1) He gave 5 talents.

2) He gave 2 talents.

3) He gave 1 talents.

The first two servants got busy and gained other talents. The third servant hid his Lord's money.

When the Master returns He commends the first two servants saying: ***"Well done, thou good and faithful servant: thou hast been faithful over a few things, I will make thee ruler over many things: enter thou into the joy of thy Lord.***

But the third servant who did nothing with what his Lord gave him heard these words: ***"Thou wicked and slothful servant…"*** ***"Take therefore the talent from him, and give it unto him which hath ten talents."*** ***"And cast ye the unprofitable servant into outer darkness: there shall be weeping and gnashing of teeth."***

We all have been given talents equaling money, but we have also been given talents; meaning gifts and the ability to use these gifts for the glory of God.

We are to serve: 1) <u>God</u>   (Romans 6:22; Hebrews 9:14)

                     2) <u>Christ</u>   (Colossians 3:24)

                     3) <u>Spirit</u>   (Romans 7:6)

We serve and work because of God's grace and the gift of His Son.

We serve and work because Jesus gave His life for us, so we can love and work for Him.

We serve and work through the leadership and love of the Spirit.

Someone once said ~ I don't work for my <u>salvation</u>.

I say <u>Amen</u> ~ We work because of <u>salvation</u>.

It's much more than work, it's a labor of love.

One day while strolling through the halls of Moody Bible Institute, I saw a picture that caught my eye and made me stop. It was a picture of a man carrying another man, sweat dropping off of the man bearing this heavy load. Another man walking by in the picture asked him:

Q. *"Isn't he heavy?"*

A. *"He's not heavy, he's my brother!"*

Folks, you and I should work not because we feel we have too, but because we want to. (Ephesians 2:8-9) ***"For by grace are ye saved through faith; and that not of yourselves: it is the gift of God:" "Not of works, lest any man should boast."***

Would you say with me ***"Amen"*** and ***"Praise the Lord."***

But it doesn't stop here, let's read the next verse. ***"For we are His workmanship, created in Christ Jesus unto good works, which God hath before ordained that we should walk in them."***

- Walk in what? <u>Good</u> works (Romans 2:10)
- We must work while it is? <u>Day</u> (John 9:4)
- If we are doers of the work we shall be blessed in our? <u>Deeds</u> (James 1:25)
- I will show you my faith by my? <u>Works</u> (James 2:18)

* Works don't produce faith, but faith always produces work.

* God help us to be excited about our Father's business.

When talking to the churches in Revelation, Jesus said something about each church that I think is worth mentioning here. He said to every single church:

"I know thy works."

It doesn't matter if man doesn't see what we do for God, because God always sees.

And you can rest assured that: **God keeps an accurate record!**

In the book: A Life God Rewards it states six main events of your forever life!

1 ~ Life   You are created in the image of God for a life of purpose.

2 ~ Death   You die physically, but not spiritually, "Yet since you are more than organic matter your life as a soul and spirit continues."

3 ~ Destination   You reach your destination after death, which is determined by what you believed on earth. "Your eternal destination is decided by whether you believed in Jesus while you were still alive." (Heaven or Hell)

4 ~ Resurrection   You receive a resurrected body. "In eternity every person will experience bodily resurrection." (John 5:28-29) Our new bodies will be immortal - they can never again experience death (I Corinthians 15).

 * 5 ~ Repayment   You receive your reward or your retribution for eternity, based on what you did on earth. "Although your eternal destination is based on your belief, how you spend eternity is based on your behavior while on earth."

This should help motivate us to work for God knowing what we do will one day be rewarded for all eternity.

6 ~ Eternity   You will live forever in the presence or absence of God, reaping the consequences of your beliefs and actions on earth.

It's a real life in a real place.

Consider this: That your actions today do have the potential to radically affect your eternity, wouldn't that dramatically change how you think about your life? How you think about God? And what you choose to do one minute from now?

144

* Eternity should hold no threat, only great promise!

If you're not a servant busy for God, don't you think it's time to start working for Him today?

Start out by praying and asking God's direction while daily reading His word. Be faithful to your church, come early, shake hands, smile and be a blessing to someone.

Ask the Pastor, deacon, or the Sunday school superintendent if there is anything you can do to help. (Be faithful.)

Be willing to do the smallest of jobs with great pleasure, knowing God is well pleased.

B) <u>WITNESS</u> (Servant)

Witness (N): 1: Testimony 2: One that gives endurance... 3: One present at a transaction so as to be able to testify that it has taken place. 4: One who has personal knowledge or experience of something. 5: Something serving as evidence or proof.

Witness (Vb): l: To bear witness: Testify. 2: To act as legal witness of. 3: To furnish proof of: betoken. 4: To be a witness of.

1. <u>We are commanded to be witnesses</u>

(Acts 1:8) ***"But ye shall receive power, after that the Holy Ghost is come upon you: and ye shall be witnesses unto me both in Jerusalem, and in all Judaea, and in Samaria, and unto the uttermost part of the earth."***

(Acts 5:32) Talking about repentance and forgiveness of sins.
"And we are His witnesses of these things..."

(Acts 10:39) Talking about how God anointed Jesus with the Holy Ghost.
"And we are witnesses of all things which He did..."

Today as you and I are to be a witness for Jesus through the power of the Holy Ghost. As a witness we are to tell and testify of our experience and knowledge of Jesus Christ. We are witnesses not only by what we say but also, and even stronger by what we do.

Some Ways to Witness

1) <u>Pray for people</u>	6) <u>Pray at meals</u>
2) <u>Testify to people</u>	7) <u>Tracts</u>
3) <u>Help people</u>	8) <u>Cards</u>
4) <u>Give to people</u>	9) <u>Visit</u> (hospitals and rest homes)
5) <u>Live for others</u>	10) <u>Many other ways!</u>

Remember when the Jews went about to kill Paul, he went to Damascus, Jerusalem, and throughout all the coasts of Judea telling them to repent.

(Acts 26:22) *"Having therefore obtained help of God, I continue unto this day, witnessing both to small and great…"*

Everywhere Paul went he was testifying and witnessing Jesus Christ.

Shouldn't our lives be a constant witness for Jesus Christ? <u>Yes</u>

(I John 5:9-10) *"If we receive the witness of men, the witness of God is greater: for this is the witness of God which He hath testified of His Son."*

"He that believeth on the Son of God hath the witness in himself…"

(Hebrews 10:15) *"Whereof the Holy Ghost also is a witness to us…"*

Through salvation we have received the Holy Ghost and He is a witness to us, so we can be a witness in this world about Jesus. The Bible says with great power gave the apostle witness also it says we shall be witnesses, a direct command to testify and witness for the one who died for us. We should pray and ask the Holy Spirit to help us to be bold in our witnessing.

<u>We Are To Witness At:</u> ✝ ✝ ✝

1. Jerusalem =	<u>Hometown</u>	(Family)	(Acts 1-7)
2. Judea =	<u>Community</u>	(Name meaning Jewish)	(Acts 8-11)
3. Samaria =	<u>Continent</u>	(Folks we don't associate with)	(Acts 8-11)
4. Earth =	<u>World Wide</u>	(Everywhere)	(Acts 11-28)

God help us to be faithful witnesses for you in this lost and dying world.

C) <u>WINNING SOULS</u> (Servant)

There is a difference between witnessing and winning souls. A witness tells others about Jesus, but a soul winner tries to get you to make a decision for Jesus. We are witnesses, but many have trouble in being a soul winner.

Every preacher who preaches the word of God and gives an invitation to accept Jesus Christ is a soul winner.

Every person who asks someone to make a decision for Jesus Christ is a soul winner.

God commands us to try and win souls.

(Proverbs 1:7) ***"The fear of the Lord is the beginning of knowledge: but fools despise wisdom and instruction."***

(Proverbs 11:30) ***"The fruit of the righteous is a tree of life; and he that winneth souls is wise."***

God says a fool will despise or hate wisdom, then God explains wisdom as winning souls.

* If we are not wise then we are <u>foolish</u>.

Why then is it so hard to ask the questions:

1. Are you saved?

2. Would you like to give your heart to the Lord? ·

Probably the number one reason is because we as humans don't like the chance of controversy or even the unknown.

I hear people say things like this:

1. *"I don't want to push them away."*

2. *"I just don't feel comfortable asking someone about their soul."*

3. *"I want to make sure the timing is right."*

4. *"I don't know enough about the Bible."*

These are just some of the many statements that we hear, but let's take a short time and address these statements.

1) They are already headed for hell, how far are you going to push them into the second or third hell? Maybe it's time someone talked to them about their eternal destiny and their need for a Saviour.

2) You and I will probably never feel completely comfortable, but it's not about our feelings it's about someone's soul. The more you talk to others about Jesus the easier it becomes.

3) Timing is very important, but many times God opens door after door only for someone to use this as an excuse. Pray and ask the Holy Spirit to give you the right words at the right time, and above all to give you boldness. If they do not accept Jesus Christ it does not mean the timing was wrong, it just means they said no to Jesus Christ. (But you have planted a seed).

4) How long have you been saved? / It's time to grow!

Even a young child can memorize (Romans 10:9-10) and (John 3:16). If you haven't memorized it yet, why don't you pray and ask God to help you?

✝ You May Help Save Someone's Life ✝
C P R = <u>Bible</u>

Paul's desire in life was seeing others saved.

(Romans 10:1) ***"Brethren, my heart's desire and prayer to God for Israel is, that they might be saved."***

Paul continued preaching and asking men, women, boys, and girls to repent of their sins and turn to Jesus Christ.

This led Paul to imprisonment, and even while being locked up continued to win souls for Jesus.

(Acts 26:27) ***"King Agrippa, believest thou the prophets? I know that thou believest."***

(VS 28) ***"Then Agrippa said unto Paul, Almost thou persuadest me to be a Christian."***

Paul goes on and says I wish you were like me meaning (saved) except for these bonds. Paul knew God's command and commission to win souls for Jesus Christ. Paul remained <u>faithful even unto the end.</u>

(II Timothy 4:7) ***"I have fought a good fight, I have finished my course, I have kept the faith:"***

- It is our job to be <u>a witness</u>.
- It is our job to be <u>a soul winner</u>.
- It is God's job to <u>save the soul of man</u>.

(Acts 2:47) ***"…And the Lord added to the church daily such as should be saved."***

It's not our job to save them, but rather to present salvation to them.

A soul winner is really one who just presents salvation to the lost.

God commands us to be soul winners, to tell others what He has done for us.

Will you be a soul winner for Him? <u>Yes</u>

Remember Jesus' statements to His disciples. (Matthew 4:19)

"And He saith unto them, Follow me, and I will make you fishers of men."

Jesus wants us to be fishers of men, soul winners in this great sea of souls.

Will you become a fisher of men, women, boys, and girls for Jesus Christ?

Spend time around someone who seems to be successful in leading others to Jesus, watch what they do and learn to become a fisher of men.

Below you will find an outline on how to help us win a soul for Christ.

<u>WINNING A SOUL TO CHRIST</u>

1. Knock loudly on the door. Introduce yourself. Speak up. Be friendly! Tell who you are and whom you represent.

2. Spend several minutes in light conversation. This is very important in "preparing the soil."

3. Ask, "If you died today, do you know that you would go to Heaven?" ("I think so.") "Let me ask you this: Are you 100% sure that, if you died today, would you go to Heaven?" ("Well, maybe not completely sure.")

4. Then ask, "Would you like to be sure?" ("Why yes, everybody wants to go to Heaven.")

5. Then say, "If I could show you how you could be sure, would you be willing to do what the Bible says to do?" ("Yes.'")

6. "There are only four things you must know in order to be sure of Heaven:

1) **You must realize that you are a sinner.** (Romans 3:10; 3:23) If all are sinners, are you a sinner? ("Yes.")

2) **You must realize that you are condemned by your sin.** (Romans 5:12; 6:23) Adam sinned and the curse of death came upon the human race. The same is true today. Complete death means the body goes back to the ground and the soul is cast into hell. (Revelation 20:14-15 may be used if needed.)

3) **You must realize that Jesus paid your debt on the cross.** (Romans 5:8) Jesus never committed a single sin. This meant that He did not deserve to die, but He did die. If He did not die for His sin, then whose sin was He dying on the cross? ("For ours.")

4) **You must realize that if you receive Jesus, you can be sure of Heaven.** (Romans 10:13) According to this verse, if you were to ask God to forgive your sins and save you, what would He do? ("He would save you.")

7. Review the main points to be sure he/she understands.

8. Ask, "If we bowed our heads for prayer, and if I would lead us in prayer as best you know how, would you be willing to take Jesus as your Savior?"

9. You pray a brief prayer, then lead him/her to pray. Help him/her with praying, if necessary, using the "Sinner's Prayer" in (Luke 18:13).

10. Ask him/her to take your hand if he/she is receiving Christ as his/her Saviour.

11. You thank the Lord for his/her decision in a brief prayer.

12. Ask, "According to the Bible (Romans 10:13) where would you go if you died today?" Give the assurance of his/her salvation. Lead him/her to see that he/she is saved.

13. Lead him/her to a public profession. (Romans 10:10-11) Get him/her to promise God he/she will come to church on Sunday. Stress the importance of going forward for Jesus Christ. Quote Matthew 10:32. Warn him/her that Satan will try to stop him/her from making a public profession of faith.

14. Go by and get him/her on Sunday morning, sit with him/her in the service, and go down the aisle with him/her. Be a friend to the new Christian. Take him/her soul winning!

Applying The Service Test

1. God's service starts in your heart, and changes the thoughts of your? ____Mind____

2. Only God has the right to judge the ____Heart____ and ____Motive____ of man according to (Matthew 7:1-2).

3. In the book The Purpose Driven Life, Chapter 34, it says that real servants serve God with a mindset of five attitudes. In number 1 = Servants think more about others than about themselves. We used the letters of joy for this pattern.

     J. ____Jesus____   O. ____Others____   Y. ____Yourself____

4. In number 5 it says: Servants think of ministry as an opportunity and not an? ____Obligation____

5. When talking about rewards we listed five crowns, please list as many of these as you can:

A. ____The Incorruptible Crown____ (I Corinthians 9:25-27)

B. ____The Crown of Rejoicing____ (I Thessalonians 2:19-20)

C. ____The Crown of Life____ (Revelation 2:10)

D. ____The Crown of Righteousness____ (II Timothy 4:8)

E. ____The Crown of Glory____ (I Peter 5:2-4)

6. We then took a look at three areas of service and the first one was? ____Work____

7. According to (Romans 2:10) we are to walk in what? ____Good Works____

    According to (John 9:4) we must work while it is? ____Day____

8. In the book "A Life God Rewards" it states six main events of the forever life. List as many as you can. *Example: A) __Life__* B) ____Death____ C) ____Destination____ D) ____Resurrection____ E) ____Repayment____ F) ____Eternity____

9. The second area of service we looked at was? ____Witness____

10. According to (Acts 1:8) we are? ____Commanded____ to be a witness.

11. The third and final area of service we looked at was? ____Winning Souls____

12. According to (Proverbs 11:30) "…he that winneth souls is…"? ____Wise____

The Definition of Worship

There are three Greek verbs translated by the one English word Worship. These words are:

1. Proskuneo: "to bow or prostrate one self in submissive lowliness and deep reverence."

2. Sebomai: "to look upon with awe."

3. Latreuo: "to render service for."

True worshippers worship the Father in spirit and in truth:

for the Father seeketh such to worship Him.

We Worship Him in all His Splendor and give Him Reverence and Praise.

We Walk with Him in this life always keeping Him the focus of our Spiritual Sight.

We Work for Him, knowing this is part of worship, and that we are to be faithful Servants.

We do Warfare for Him, knowing we are to be Spiritual Soldiers.

Let's: "Fight the Good Fight of Faith"

As good soldiers and great servants of Jesus Christ

Let's suit up for battle, and be a witness and a

soul winner for Jesus Christ. (Ephesians 6:11-18)

Chapter IX

SUMMARY

I. <u>Salvation</u>

We started out in Chapter I by learning about our salvation. Realizing the work of the Father, the Son and the Holy Spirit.

Realizing that we are saved by grace through faith, and that the blood of Jesus is royal blood with full power to cleanse us from our sins.

The Old Testament blood of bulls, goats, pigeons and doves was only a temporary solution and could only cover sin.

Praise God Jesus said on the cross *"It is finished"* meaning the eternal plan of salvation for all mankind. It is a universal call to anyone and everyone who will come to Him by faith and accept this gift. I pray that you are saved and that this book has helped you to grow in the grace and knowledge of our Lord and Saviour, Jesus Christ.

We learned that the Holy Spirit is a real person and not just a force or power or given in portions as some teach. The Holy Spirit has <u>a mind</u>, <u>a will</u>, <u>He forbids</u>, <u>He permits</u>, <u>He loves</u>, <u>He grieves</u>, <u>He prays</u>, <u>He is the comforter</u> of whom Jesus spoke of, who He would send to not only be with us, but to live in us.

We then looked over the vocabulary of salvation such as <u>remission</u>, <u>redemption</u>, <u>regeneration</u>, <u>reconciliation</u>, <u>propitiation</u>, <u>preservation</u>, <u>justification</u> and the list goes on.

Then we read where once we are saved that old things are to pass away; and behold all things are to become new.

Now that you are saved it's time to go to church for praise and worship.

II. Sanctuary

We studied the Sanctuary as our <u>bodies</u>, <u>brethren</u>, being believers and the <u>building</u>. We went from the <u>Tabernacle</u> to the <u>Temple</u> to the <u>Synagogue</u> to the building being the <u>Church</u> today.

We went over our day of worship being the Lord's day (Sunday).

We then looked at the importance and purpose of the church.

Which is to: A) <u>Love God</u>

B) <u>Evangelize the World</u>

C) <u>Minister the Ordinances</u>

D) <u>Care for its Own</u>

E). <u>Fellowship</u>

F) <u>Fight the Enemy</u>

G) <u>Glorify God</u>

(Hebrews 10:25) ***"Not forsaking the assembling of ourselves together, as the manner of some is; but exhorting one another: and so much the more, as ye see the day approaching."***

(Psalms 122:1) ***"I was glad when they said unto me, Let us go into the house of the Lord."***

We should not only be faithful, but we should be excited to go and worship the Lord in His house.

III. Supplication

Prayer is one of the most important things in a Christian's life.

Prayer is the way we talk to God and is one of the two parts of communication.

Prayer is what turns those in captivity free and is so precious that it is placed into a golden vial.

Our prayers are to be addressed to the <u>Father</u> in the <u>Holy Spirit</u> and in the Name of the Son, <u>Jesus Christ</u>. For no man can come to the Father but by His Son Jesus Christ.

We are to pray <u>continually</u> in <u>faith</u> believing that God hears and answers our prayers.

We should: A = <u>Ask</u>   (Matthew 7:7-8)

              S = <u>Seek</u>

              K = <u>Knock</u>

We should ask with <u>simplicity,</u> seek with <u>intensity</u> and knock with <u>persistency</u>.

As Christians, we are to pray everywhere and always without ceasing.

IV. <u>Scriptures</u>

We first must decide if we believe in the <u>inspired, inerrant,</u> and <u>infallible</u> Word of God in <u>Greek, Hebrew, Latin,</u> and <u>English</u>.

Always remember the <u>Holy Bible</u> was given by a <u>Holy God</u> and written by <u>Holy men</u> who were led by the <u>Holy Ghost</u> to write about a <u>Holy Saviour</u> to save sinners and create <u>Holy People</u>. The Scripture is the way God talks to us and is one of the two parts of communication. This is God's love letter to us written in the blood of His only begotten Son Jesus Christ, who loved us and died for us.

The Scriptures can change a sinner into a saint, an alcoholic into a sober man, and an abusing father into a loving dad.

Through the Scriptures, we can become <u>soldiers, servants, saints, pilgrims, ambassadors, fighters, runners, farmers, brethren</u>…

Our faith comes from God's Word. (Romans 10:17) Heaven and earth shall pass away but God's Word will never pass away. One day we will be judged by what's written in the books.

        1) <u>Book of Life</u>   2) <u>Book of Deeds</u>   3) <u>The Bible</u>

V. <u>Submersion</u>

Now that you are saved, one of the first steps in obedience to following Jesus is to be baptized. (Matthew 28:18-20) <u>Known as the Great Commission!</u>

We are to go and teach and preach the gospel baptizing the believers in the name of the Father, and of the Son, and of the Holy Ghost.

This we do as an outward symbol and a sign of what has taken place on the inside.

This is one of the three ordinances of the church.

1) <u>The Lord's Supper</u>   2) <u>Feet Washing</u>   3) <u>Baptism</u>

If you have not been baptized since you have been saved, ask your pastor to baptize you. This is the first step in following Jesus in this new journey we have now begun.

VI. <u>Stewardship</u>

We then went on to stewardship and how we use our time for eternity.

We went over the gifts given in (Romans 12):

1) <u>Preaching</u>   2) <u>Serving</u>   3) <u>Teaching</u>   4) <u>Exhorter</u>

5) <u>Giving</u>   6) <u>Organizer</u>   7) <u>Mercy</u>

We were given a test to learn our primary gift so we can use it for the glory of God.

We then went onto learn the blessing of money and the importance of out tithes and offerings to God. The secret is realizing it's all God's money, and then it becomes an instrument in the hands of a faithful steward. The love of money is the root of all evil, and if we live to make money for ourselves, we then become a slave to it. God help us to be good faithful stewards with what You have blessed us with.

VII. <u>Sanctification</u>

To purify, separate, cleanse from corruption, consecrate, to make holy and pure.

We are sanctified by God in the Holy Ghost and in Christ Jesus. We are placed in <u>sanctification</u> through <u>salvation</u>. This is called <u>Positional Sanctification</u>. Then of course there is <u>Processional Sanctification</u> as we die daily to things in our lives. This will bring us to a place called <u>Personal Sanctification</u> where we make Jesus our Saviour now our Lord and Master.

This is called a place of perfection or completion in Jesus Christ. This is the place as a Christian where we see God begins to do great miracles in our lives. There should be an average maturing period of around three years where we are to be able to start eating the meat of the Word of God. We should be used as vessels unto honor seeking always His will above our own.

This life is also called a life of holiness.

VIII. Service

We are to be faithful servants in the service of our Lord and Master Jesus Christ.

True service will bring joy to the Christian's life.

    J = Jesus

    O = Others

    Y = Yourself

If we keep this joy of serving in the right order God will be magnified and we will be blessed.

According to (Mark 10:28-30) we will be blessed and rewarded for our work here on earth.

According to (I Corinthians 9:25-27; Revelation 2:10...) we will be blessed and rewarded when we get to heaven. Though satan, sinner, and self can strip us from our rewards, we must be constant in our walk of service.

Remember: Salvation is Free ~ Discipleship will cost you!

Are you willing to pay the price and follow Jesus Christ no matter what? (I pray that you are.) My aim and prayer is that this book has been a blessing, and a building of your faith. I pray this has taken you down the road to help you reach spiritual maturity, and become a disciple of Christ.

(II Peter 3:18)

"But grow in grace, and in the knowledge
of our Lord and Saviour Jesus Christ.
To Him be glory both now and forever.
Amen."

www.ingramcontent.com/pod-product-compliance
Lightning Source LLC
Chambersburg PA
CBHW081212020426
42331CB00012B/3002